IN THE TIME OF THE RIGHT

Reflections on Liberation

Suzanne Pharr

Chardon Press

1 2 3 4 5 6 2001 2000 1999 1998 1997 1996

Cover and book design by Deborah Dudley
Back cover photo by Rebecca G. Carey

Published by Chardon Press
Berkeley, California

Distributed by the Women's Project
2224 Main Street
Little Rock, AR 72206

Library of Congress Catalog Card Number: 96-084155

ISBN 0-9620222-8-4

ACKNOWLEDGMENTS

This book was written with the partnership and collaboration of many people. I want to thank the following colleagues/friends/loved ones for their thoughtful comments on the manuscript: Chip Berlet, Renée DeLapp, Virginia Fuqua, Suzanne Goldberg, Jean Hardisty, Kerry Lobel, Judy Matsuoka, Pam McMichael, Melinda Pittman, Beth Richie, Eric Rofes, Jane Sapp, Mab Segrest, Barbara Smith, Frieda Takamura, Urvashi Vaid, Carmen Vazquez, and Thalia Zepatos.

Chardon Press' publishing and editing team of Kim Klein and Nancy Adess was dynamic and supportive. Deborah Dudley's careful editing, layout, and design was a gift, and her humor, generous spirit, broad literary and political understanding made her a joy to work with.

Renée DeLapp kept me going by providing loving attention to the details that constitute full support: finding a beautiful cabin for sabbatical writing time, reading the manuscript again and again, challenging and talking through difficult ideas, providing good fun and good food.

The staff and board of the Women's Project, as always, gave me their strong support to find a voice for the work we do.

THE WOMEN'S PROJECT

The Women's Project, working for social and economic justice since 1981, uses educational and organizing strategies to create a world free of discrimination, violence, and economic injustice.

Profits from IN THE TIME OF THE RIGHT: *Reflections on Liberation* are used for funding the work of the Women's Project.

Much of the material in this book appeared in articles published in *Transformation*, a newsletter of political analysis and opinion, one of the benefits of a $25 membership in the Women's Project.

Additional copies of IN THE TIME OF THE RIGHT: *Reflections on Liberation* may be ordered from

Women's Project
2224 Main Street
Little Rock, Arkansas 72206

Phone: 501/372-5113
Fax: 501/372-0009
e-mail: wproject@aol.com

The Women's Project also distributes *Homophobia: A Weapon of Sexism* by Suzanne Pharr.

*Dedicated to those who support democracy through
seeking justice and equality—*

*And in memory of Ann Gallmeyer (1945-1995) who
taught us that physical disability cannot
restrain the indomitable spirit
of those who love freedom.*

is most disturbing is that so many people feel overwhelmed, having concluded they have no way of gaining control of their lives and communities, of changing bad things to the better. Hope diminishes. There is a marked increase in those responding to the appeals evangelicals make to mass audiences, in those seeking spiritual healers, in those pursuing mysticism and the occult.

In this climate, those offering simplistic and authoritarian answers find easy targets for their fundraising, organizing and constituency-building. Social chaos, along with our fears that we cannot achieve social stability, can be heightened to overshadow the need for change in the current economic structure. Thus we have seen the rapid rise of the Right, particularly the religious Right, providing answers that eliminate choice, reduce complexity, and offer fundamentalist authoritarianism as a means of acquiring social stability.

This small book offers some ways to understand what is happening in this country. It is a call for action to all concerned people who are searching for new choices in our efforts to find better ways to live with each other; choices that move us toward liberation and freedom rather than domination and authoritarianism. It represents only a beginning, an offer of some ideas to provoke critical thinking. This volume is written for people, especially those involved in progressive social change work, who have a passion for justice and equality. It is for those whose instincts are to relieve suffering, to end bigotry, to share fairly, to live as good neighbors—yes, to follow the Golden Rule ("Do unto others...") on the individual, community and national levels. It is for those who have felt the depths of injustice inflicted upon Native Americans, upon enslaved people from Africa, upon Europe's Jews, sweatshop workers, peoples whose lands have been made toxic, the indigenous peoples of Nicaragua, the black South Africans, the mining people of Appalachia, the comfort women of Korea—and who have thought, "There is great injustice here, and I stand with them, on their side."

This book is for those who, like myself, are searching for a way to make positive change. It is for people who are not sure of the answers but know that, with the help of others, answers can be found. It is an affirmation of my belief that change is constantly occurring, and our choices determine whether change is progressive and liberating or regressive and fascistic.

This book is based on my belief that people are not innately good or bad, but that societal and cultural forces influence who we are, and that we as individuals and communities can help shape those forces for good or bad. I contend that people must have valid information, political education, and a wide variety of choices. I reaffirm the idea that everyone can change, and change rapidly, if given opportunities.

I draw my hope for change from my own life, most of which has been dedicated to progressive social change. My Southern rural family and community did not offer a window into progressive politics, and I have been a slow learner on the political path. I offer my life as an example—that is, if I could change and grow politically, maybe anyone could.

As a kid raised on a dirt farm in Georgia in the 1940s and 1950s, I was ready for information and guidance to attack the injustice I saw and felt. I wanted to change the world but had no models other than missionaries. I went back and forth between wanting to be a missionary and feeling devastating outrage and fury at the organized church that preached the inferiority of black Americans. Rebellious and anarchic, I knew something was terribly wrong but did not know what to do except to lash out, usually without much thought, whenever I experienced unfairness.

I found no guidance in school. In addition to economic poverty, I also experienced educational poverty, which was far worse. I spent three years of high school English classes benumbed as we read the *Reader's Digest* educational series. Each day we read an article from the *Reader's Digest* and answered the questions printed at the end. No interaction occurred between teacher and students, no dialogue among students. When I entered a small rural women's college, I was astounded to meet people who had studied novels and poetry in their high school classes. My own intellectual life had been fed at home almost entirely by the *Saturday Evening Post*, and I had read novels on my own, thanks to the monthly visits of my beloved county bookmobile.

I entered college in 1957, a farm kid who had read novels and watched a little television but who had not heard the word "homosexual" until it was used to describe me at age 18. In pain and outrage, I beat my fists bloody against my dormitory door. I had been in love with my high school girlfriend and had also dated boys throughout high school, and I could not understand this word used in degradation and disgust to describe the person I was. It was a word that waited to ambush me at every turn throughout my years at a tiny Georgia women's college.

I had heard of the 1954 Supreme Court decision in *Brown v. Board of Education* and knew only enough to join a few others in protesting the state of Georgia's plans to close schools to keep them segregated. But mostly I didn't see much beyond the narrow circumference of my life. I thought a hot little high school basketball player who was voted best all around and best personality in her class could make her way any place she tried—even if she was ignorant as sin, even if she was a closeted lesbian.

As the 1960s opened the great roiling period of social change, I had nothing to prepare me but a passion for a few writers (Wordsworth, Keats, Thoreau, and Faulkner), a belief that we would all die from an atomic bomb before I was 30, and a sense that something was wrong with our society. Swinging from idea to idea, political position to political position, I did not know if I could rest in the camp of Civil Rights leader Martin Luther King, Jr., or right-wing Senator Barry Goldwater, or anti-racist writer Lillian Smith, or super-individualistic novelist Ayn Rand. All passionate people who offered some vision of change were appealing.

How then did I find a path to the choice of social justice work for a life's vocation as a community organizer and a political writer, a feminist and anti-racist worker?

A compass was handed to me by people along the way who believed that true participatory democracy could be created in this country and that I could be part of its creation. They thought that people working together could help shape the destiny of the nation, could create a movement made up of the oppressed, the exploited, the silenced. They reached out to me. They listened to my ideas and challenged them, accepted my reality, let me make mistakes, talked and argued and debated with me, put up with me, but always held me to my best self and best work. I remember, for example, Elizabeth Rogers in New Orleans in the early 1970s, who in her 80s was attending women's liberation meetings. Having spent her life organizing for workers' rights, she introduced me to the history of the union movement which I had never been taught in schools, and she encouraged me to think about which side I stood on in economic struggles. Evangeline K. Brown, an Arkansas warrior of the Civil Rights Movement, taught me that I must commit to a lifetime of struggle for justice, pacing myself for endurance and survival.

In particular, women of color gave me the opportunity to learn. I have come to believe it is always a gift when someone gives another the space to make mistakes and learn. After hundreds of years of white supremacy, I believe it is an act of grace when people of color give white people a second chance and do not just discard us as well-meaning but ignorant and harmful.

Many people in my life have offered me an invitation that is a gift: to work in solidarity with them to create a better world.

This book is for those who believe in progressive change for all of us. For those who are willing to talk with people different from themselves. For those willing to listen to those most often silenced. For those who believe in our common humanity and our common good. For those who want to work with others for the liberation of us all and who fear the domination and exclusion promoted by the Right. For those who believe in the great moral values of justice, equality, and freedom—this book is an invitation.

THE RISE OF THE RIGHT

Though now entrenched in the political mainstream, the Right has not always been taken seriously. However, over the past three decades they were developing strategies and building a base. There were many signs of their increasing presence and strength, but many of them were unrecognized or discounted by progressive people.

For the past few years I have spent most of my time thinking about, writing about, and speaking about the rise of the Right, particularly the theocratic Right (often called the religious Right) whose goal is the merger of church and state and the creation of a government ruled by officials who claim divine authority from a Christian god. I have also spent time berating myself for underestimating the scope of their plan and not acknowledging where their burgeoning power was headed until they were armed with a well-greased propaganda machine and dangerous. Now, what was once considered the "extremist" Right can no longer be considered extremist: it has come to occupy the middle ground of U.S. politics, influencing every sphere of public and private life.

For many, it now seems that the Right suddenly emerged full blown on the national scene in the 1980s. I invite each reader to look back reflectively over the past decade or so to events that foreshadowed our current political environment. Each of our own experiences contains political truth. Sometimes we do not comprehend its meaning until there is a critical mass of information and we can recognize the linkages. Beginning in the 1970s, examples from my own experiences with the Right show how insidiously and strategically they have implemented a comprehensive agenda in a piecemeal fashion. Today's right-wing themes and arguments flow throughout these experiences.

• In 1976, while I was living with six women on a farm in northwest Arkansas, in the days of back-to-the-land simplicity and collective experimentation, we learned that feminists in Little Rock would host a statewide women's conference to help develop the platform to be presented at the Houston International Year of the Woman Conference the following year. We also heard that the organizers did not want lesbians to attend because Phyllis Schlafly of the Eagle Forum was bringing in busloads of women from other states to dominate each of these conferences throughout the South. One of her main issues was that feminists were anti-men, anti-family lesbians. We were less concerned about Phyllis Schlafly than the fact that the local organizers might give in to the fear of the Eagle Forum's irrational, homophobic thinking. A carload of us lesbians (commonly known as "a bunch of...") drove down from the Ozark mountains to Little Rock where we confronted the organizers and gained a recognized place at the conference.

Later that day I bought Skipper, a black and white rat terrier puppy. This dog survived all the tales I tell here to die 17 years later in Portland, Oregon, in the middle of the 1992 "No on 9" campaign to defeat the anti-gay and lesbian ballot measure. The events surrounding this dog's life and death became markers for how rapidly the Right has worked. In only 17 years, the theocratic Right evolved from being the sometimes laughable, militant fringe to joining other sectors of the Right and becoming a mighty force in legislatures, Congress, fundamentalist and mainstream churches, think tanks, schools, and every institution where public policy is made. Beginning in the 1970s with attacks against *Roe v. Wade*, the gains of the Civil Rights Movement, gender and racial equality, and lesbians and gay men, the Right's power has grown to such a point that now, in the mid-1990s, civil rights, civil liberties, and democracy itself are threatened. All in the lifetime of one little black and white dog.

• In 1977, Anita Bryant, the orange juice advertising queen, hit the headlines with her "Save the Children" attacks against lesbians and gay men in Florida, using similar strategies to those developed in the 1973 San Francisco initiative to ban gay teachers from the classroom. The same year, I began work as director of Washington County Head Start in Fayetteville, Arkansas and joined a group of 15 women who came together to develop a shelter for battered women. I became the chair of the shelter's board as a visible lesbian, and a few months later (now 1978, the year San Francisco's gay political leader Harvey Milk and Mayor George Moscone were murdered), my boss was calling for me to be fired from Head Start because I "was a lesbian and proud of it." This experience foreshadowed the Right's argument that to talk about homosexuality is to recruit others "into" homosexuality. Many of my co-workers and many of the parents of Head Start children took high-risk, principled positions supporting me during this six-month attack, which included public hearings and anonymous death threats. I weathered it and kept my job.

• In 1981, just after Ronald Reagan was elected, the Family Protection Act was submitted to Congress. Fortunately, thanks to the hard work of many progressive people, it was defeated. In hindsight I realize that we should have paid even closer attention to its content and, after its defeat, to the strategy used to bring about its reinvention and eventual victory.

The most criticized aspects of the bill were that, through a states' rights strategy, it would prohibit federal regulation of activities or programs that were directly or indirectly operated by church or religious organizations; prohibit federal intervention in cases of child abuse, spouse abuse, and juvenile delinquency; prohibit the use of federal funds for any group that "presents homosexuality as an acceptable lifestyle;" prohibit the use of federal funds in schools that use textbooks that do not show women in their "traditionally defined roles;" prohibit abortion or contraceptive information for teenagers without their parents' consent; provide tax breaks for church-operated schools; reaffirm corporal punishment of children by teachers; give a tax exemption of $1000 to *married* parents who have a child; prohibit the federally funded Legal Services program from handling cases having to do with divorce, abortion, or homosexual rights; and prohibit federal funding to any state that prohibits voluntary prayer on the premises of any public building.

When the Family Protection Act failed to pass Congress, its supporters vowed to break it into separate pieces and pass it piece by piece in the years to come. They put the country on notice and then set out to accomplish the task. Some of the pieces are now in place; others are currently on the Right's agenda in the Republican-controlled 104th Congress.

• In 1981, I founded the Women's Project, a nonprofit community organization that uses a multi-issue approach to social change. Focusing on the elimination of racism and sexism, it works primarily in the areas of economics and violence against women and children. When first seeking funding from foundations in 1980, I was warned that Reagan's election would bring about harsh attacks against social justice organizations and that I should think about incorporating under

3

the auspices of a church. Remembering the long history of the United Methodist Church in fighting injustice, especially in the South, I asked them to be the fiscal agent for the project. Attacks from the "Good News" (or conservative Right) Methodists began almost immediately. Despite the church contributing less than $5,000 a year to the Women's Project, a couple of pastors who had never met me or any of our board and staff demanded each year that the Church disassociate itself from us because of our lesbian leadership. Today, 15 years later, these "Good News" ministers still make the same demand every year, despite the fact that the Church has not been our fiscal agent for 10 years (though it still gives us a small amount of money and United Methodist Women participate in our program of transporting the children of women prisoners to visit their mothers each month). The most famous "Good News" minister is Donald Wildmon, head of the right-wing American Family Association which has been one of the foremost proponents of censorship of the arts and a major adversary of any positive recognition of lesbians and gay men.

• In 1982, I went to my first conference on battered women sponsored by the National Coalition Against Domestic Violence (NCADV) in Milwaukee, Wisconsin. At that conference, the Lesbian Task Force, seeking a visible lesbian in the shelter movement to try to deal with the attacks from both within and without the movement occurring against lesbian workers, elected me as its chair. Of far greater import, though, was the controversy that arose from two conference events and gave rise to a reaction about race and homosexuality that the Right has since incorporated in its appeal to white heterosexuals.

On the day before the full conference began, there was an institute for women of color, attended only by women of color, where issues pertaining specifically to them were discussed. This was quite a new idea for those days, and we were all excited that more than 100 women attended, out of a conference of about 1200. Most of us white women had never witnessed such group dynamism and power among women of color as when they emerged from a full day of talking and building solidarity with each other. It was clearly a new day, a new vision. Equally surprising—and disturbing for some—was the list of resolutions that the group presented to the conference, because among them was a solidarity resolution supporting the struggles of lesbians in the movement.

The second controversial event was that the tiny lesbian task force (perhaps 8-10 women) had asked lesbians and their allies to show their support by wearing pink triangles at the conference. Perhaps 50 women wore them.

From these two small groups—100 women of color talking solidarity and 50 lesbians and their allies wearing pink triangles (some of whom belonged in both groups)—came the raging controversy. White women began to rumble, "The movement has been taken over by women of color and lesbians. There's no room for white women any more." (Here was the attitude—"someone's taking something from me"—that the Right would exploit more thoroughly a decade later.) They took that message home to their state battered women's coalitions, and those coalitions began calling in complaints to the National Coalition, with a few threatening to withdraw from the NCADV altogether.

The Lesbian Task Force of the NCADV responded by sending a team of one lesbian and one heterosexual to speak with two of the coalitions, Louisiana and Mississippi, that were threatening to withdraw. As chair, I went with two different members of the NCADV steering committee to each of these states. Our agreement was that we would not announce ourselves as a lesbian/heterosexual team—we would let them think what they wished—and the heterosexual team member would not affirm or deny heterosexuality as part of her credentials. Our goal was to listen and to offer information about lesbians and women of color in the battered women's movement and the importance of their participation. We listened to arguments about the sickness and sin of lesbians, about how the presence of lesbians on staff or as residents would destroy shelters, and how our work was to deal with violence against women, not racism and homophobia.

When we debriefed those visits, each of the heterosexual women on the team said she had never felt so verbally assaulted, that she did not realize such ignorance of and bias toward homosexuality existed, nor that white heterosexuals felt so threatened by lesbians and women of color. From this experience, we learned that arguments supporting the issues of lesbians and women of color were too complex to present comprehensively in a single visit to a local program. Another lesson we learned is that educational work that is counter to the long-held beliefs of the dominant culture has to be introduced over time and in ways that give people the opportunity to think about and discuss new ideas thoroughly.

• In 1985, the Department of Justice (DOJ) asked the NCADV to submit a grant proposal to create a national education campaign about violence against women. After some debate about the politics of accepting money from the DOJ (never a friend of battered women), a grant proposal for $600,000 was written and submitted. Almost immediately, the Heritage Foundation, a prestigious right-wing think tank, took its objections to our project to the media, calling the NCADV a "pro-lesbian, pro-feminist, anti-family organization." The DOJ, led at that time by Edwin Meese, then withdrew the offer of a grant and instead offered a "cooperative agreement" which gave them final authority over all of our materials and media work.

After a prolonged and emotionally charged debate, the steering committee of the NCADV moved, by a fragile consensus, to accept the DOJ's terms. Then we entered an eight-month struggle with the DOJ over the inclusion of discussion of lesbian battering and racism in our materials. At the end of yet another painful, divisive debate, the steering committee agreed that we could not live with the contradiction; that by accepting the DOJ's power and control over our beliefs and activities we were going against our deepest principles. We were in conflict with our own analysis of battering: that violence and oppression come from the desire and ability of the perpetrators to exert power and control over their victims. We rejected the DOJ's money, but rather than this action unifying us, the NCADV and state coalitions were rent asunder by the conflicts among ourselves over the decision. This led, I believe, to the demise of a national, centralized battered women's movement.

The divisions paralleled those that emerged after the 1982 NCADV conference. There were those who believed that battering occurs within a context of other oppressions, such as sexism, homophobia, racism, economic injustice, and that to end the violence we must understand and work to change all of these. Others, however, believed that the issue was simply the battering of women and our primary responsibility was to provide services to victims. At the heart of the conflict was the question of whether our work should be simply service delivery which, like charity, leaves power structures unchallenged, or should expand beyond service delivery to social change, which includes working against all oppressions so that violence against all women can be stopped.

• In 1988, I initiated a program at the Women's Project called the Women's Watchcare Network. Its purpose is to monitor and maintain anecdotal documentation of the activities of the white supremacist Right and the theocratic Right as well as individual acts of biased violence (commonly known as hate violence) against people of religious minorities, people of color, women, lesbians and gay men. From its beginning, the project was controversial because it includes women as targets of biased violence. Our argument is supported by the fact that each year we document between 60 and 90 murders, many of which are extraordinarily vicious, of women by men in Arkansas.

In 1991, we documented a controversial act of sexist violence and held a press conference about it. Just before they were due to go to the Final Four playoffs, the championship University of Arkansas Razorback basketball team, all of whom were black players, gang-raped a young, drunk white woman who had been dancing in a bar and then returned home with them. The press jumped to defend the young men and condemn the woman. In our press conference, we responded to what we considered a very complex situation with a complex response. We asserted that rape is wrong and that no one, no matter what her behavior, deserves to be raped. However, we also talked about how young black men in Arkansas are sought for university life when they are high school basketball stars, how they are discarded when they are no longer productive players, and how their negative behavior is condoned or overlooked only when they are sports stars. Otherwise, it is racism as usual, and they are seen as sexual predators and economic and social problems.

Controversy about race and gender raged around the incident, and the Women's Project was attacked again and again by the *Arkansas Democrat*'s right-wing editorialist, Robert Starr, who released the name of the victim and criticized us for interjecting race into the issue and for defending the victim. By the end of the conflict, our stack of newspaper clippings was three inches high, and our stand had highlighted not only racism and sexism in the state, but a division between the black community and the white women's community; each of them criticized us, the former for our position on gender, the latter for our position on race.

• In 1991, I was asked to give a speech in Kansas City about the Women's Watchcare Network. At that time I was developing an analysis about how biased murders of gay men are similar to hate murders of women. When I arrived in town, my hosts told me that two members of FIRED-UP (Freedom Involves Responsibly Exposing Decadence and Upholding Principle) had condemned me on their radio show and were planning to attend my speech. At the time, I thought these women operated with smoke and mirrors since it seemed there were only two of them in the organization, yet they were having significant success in opposing abortion, raising a fuss about school curricula, and attacking the lives of lesbians and gay men. They had learned how to use the media, especially radio. Though not Rush Limbaughs by any means, they had found a responsive audience and were doing the effective grassroots work to organize supporters—work that soon thousands across the country would replicate.

• In the fall of 1991, at the annual Creating Change conference of the National Gay and Lesbian Task Force, two political workers from Oregon showed me a videotape entitled "The Gay Agenda," featuring Lon Mabon of the Oregon Citizens Alliance (OCA), which depicted lesbians and gay men as sexual predators seeking civil rights. Upon seeing it and hearing about the OCA's "No Special Rights" ballot initiative, I suspected the Right was using Oregon as a national test site in its strategy to alter or prohibit civil rights through constitutional amendments. After talking with others at the conference, I learned that Colorado was targeted also.

• In January 1992, I went to Oregon to work for eight months with local activists and organizers in an effort to frame what was happening there within a larger national context. I asserted then and still very much believe that what was happening in Oregon was not simply a specific attack against lesbians and gay men, but an attack on democracy itself. It was in this work with the people of Oregon, two thousand miles from the South where I had lived and worked my whole life among many conservatives as well as the far Right, that I was able to witness firsthand the collective forces of the theocratic Right, the far Right and the more elusive corporate Right.

A MAJOR MOVEMENT

It was in Oregon, finally, that I came to recognize that this is a well-organized army on the march. Why, I asked myself, had I failed to connect the dots between the many signs of the build-up? Not just the ones directly involved in my own life, but the others: the anti-gay and lesbian Briggs Initiative, the anti-property tax Proposition 13, the "reverse discrimination" *Bakke* decision in California, the anti-abortion street wars of Operation Rescue, the anti-Equal Rights Amendment campaigns, the attacks on labor unions and workers, the greed and divisiveness that were emerging all around me?

Like many other people, I was working on a dozen fronts at once and failing to see the big picture. I was busy trying to put out brush fires among the trees rather than seeing that the entire forest was about to be clear-cut. Also, I was framing the conflict as one between conservatives and liberals, with us progressives trying to define and defend core issues focused on race, class, and gender.

When I considered the Right, I thought of it as made up of distinct groups. The most dangerous was what seemed to be a corporate Right, that during most of the 1980s I viewed as economic conservatives who were filled with greed but not necessarily turning toward an ideological Right. The far Right was clearly on my radar as primarily an influential, white supremacist defining edge, shaping the parameters of bigotry and violence. As for the theocratic Right, I was one among many who did not take them very seriously, who, in fact, saw them as buffoons on the fringe appealing to those who put emotion before thought and sought simple solutions as salvation in a world of complex problems that were overwhelming them. I was not a researcher, I was a social justice organizer—I saw the Right through a fractured lens as they entered my everyday organizing experience, and I did not see their connected, mutual interests.

It was in Oregon that I set myself the task of focusing on the rise of the Right (not, as before, on violence against women and children, discrimination against identity groups, AIDS education, biased violence, incarcerated women, and economic injustice), and when I did, the pieces began to fall into place.

Even in 1992 during the major onslaught from the Right in so many places across the nation, many of us still did not understand their power nor how fast they could put it in place and use it. Perhaps the 1992 elections misled us as we watched what seemed to be the victory of the Right at the Republican National Convention and their subsequent defeat at the polls with the election of Bill Clinton. At that time, we were more assured there was a debate, that the middle of U.S. politics could be struggled over, that the Right could be turned back handily by a generation of baby boomers and politically organized identity groups, that the working class and poor would rise up. Very few predicted how fast right-wing ideology would move into the mainstream or recognized this political force for the steamroller it was.

Who would have thought that two years after the 1992 elections Republican conservatives and right wingers would take over the Republican Party and sweep victoriously through both the House and Senate as well as through many local legislatures? That there would be ballot initiatives to limit the civil rights of immigrants, lesbians and gay men, and one called the "Civil Rights Initiative" designed to eliminate affirmative action? That the Supreme Court would begin moving us backward decades by unraveling civil rights and liberties? That there would be a strong move toward the privatization of public lands and the elimination of regulations protecting workers and the environment? That the Democratic Party, abandoning its traditional base and moving toward business interests, would have almost fallen apart? That Aid to Families with Dependent Children and almost every other federally-funded program designed to meet human needs would be on the verge of being defunded? That the U.S. would embrace a return to states' rights? That the civil liberties and civil rights guaranteed in the Constitution would be in jeopardy? That there would be a major social change movement, indeed a revolution, in place and it would belong not to the Left but to the Right?

DOMINATION POLITICS

Movements grow from the beliefs and desires of large groups of people. The Right has found fertile ground in the attitudes of ordinary people, many of whom do not support the Right's agenda but who nevertheless hold beliefs that give it room to grow.

How did the Right bring about this revolution? For any group to gain power, people must give them access to power, either knowingly or unknowingly. The rise to power does not occur in a vacuum; large numbers of people are usually complicit with it, either through action or inaction, through support or silence. The Right has gained power by placing wedges along the existing societal faultlines of race, class, gender, and sexuality and expanding them into larger divisions. The Right has gained power because it has found a fertile place to grow in the current beliefs and attitudes of the people of this land. This growth has occurred because ordinary citizens have supported individual and institutional politics of domination.

Dominator. Colonizer. Supremacist. Oppressor. Imperialist. These names are interrelated. They describe individuals, groups, and countries that seek power and control over the lives of others.

I believe there are two kinds of politics: the politics of domination and the politics of liberation. With the former, the few seek to have power over the lives of the many, gaining it through systems of oppression and exploitation. With the latter, the goal is for the many to share decision-making, resources and responsibilities for the good of the group as well as the individual. These politics operate on both the individual and public institutional levels. This chapter will explore the politics of domination, the following will give an example of the rise of the Right from this foundation, and the final chapter will present examples of liberation politics.

Domination politics begin with a belief in meritocracy. Meritocracy is the belief that a culture already provides the level playing field that Jesse Jackson mentions in his speeches as a dream yet to come true. Because everyone, despite one's race, class, or gender, is thought to have equal access to achievement, one's success or failure is understood to be earned, deserved, or merited ("if she'd only worked harder, she wouldn't be poor") and a result of innate qualities (e.g., muscle, will power, intelligence), not social or cultural structures. From this belief comes a conviction that some people are superior to others and therefore are justified in their efforts to control the lesser folks and to reap the benefits of their labors. In this country, domination politics are founded on the belief that the rich are superior to the poor, men superior to women, white people to people of color, Christians to Jews and other religious minorities, heterosexuals to lesbians and gay men, able-bodied people to people with disabilities.

The last decade provided a fine example of the solidification of domination politics and the surge of economic injustice, oppression, and moral bankruptcy. Not since the 1920s had there been such an increase in economic inequality as there was in the 1980s, the Reagan/Bush years. From 1983-1989, the nation's wealth increased by $2.8 trillion. The top *0.5%* of families gained 54%, the next 9.5% gained 36.%, and the remainder of us (90 % of U.S. families) received *only 9.7%* of this incredible increase in wealth. (Lawrence Mishel and Jared Bernstein, *State of Working America 1994-95*, New York: M.E. Sharpe, 1994, p. 247) This increase in wealth and its grossly unequal distribution continue today, brought to even greater extremes by the tax and regulatory policies of the Republican-controlled Congress, unchecked and often supported by "centrist" Democrats.

The distance between the rich and the poor widened enormously as conservatives gave tax breaks to the rich, reducing the tax on the richest Americans from 70% to 28%, the same rate as middle income people are taxed. What is meant by "the richest Americans?" During the decade, the number of millionaires rose from 574,000 to 1.3 million; billionaires, from a few to 52—all taxed the same as those who make $45,000 a year. While the incomes of the bottom 10% of the population fell by 10.5%, the incomes of the top 10% rose by 24.4%, and the incomes of the top 1% rose by a staggering 74.2%. And the national debt tripled. (*Politics of Rich and Poor*, Kevin Phillips, Random House, 1990)

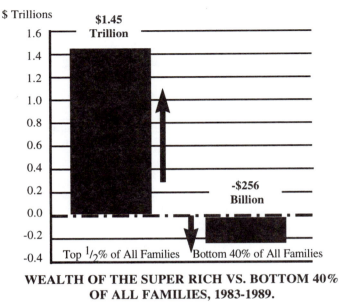

**WEALTH OF THE SUPER RICH VS. BOTTOM 40%
OF ALL FAMILIES, 1983-1989.**
From: *Corporate Power and the American Dream*, The Labor
Institute, NY, NY.

Obscene greed and luxury consumption became the standard for
rich stockholders as corporations sought greater wealth from increased
profit margins gained by cutting back salaries and benefits, downsizing,
eliminating full-time employees and taking on part-time workers; moving companies abroad to exploit even cheaper labor; finding every tax
loophole and creating new ones; buying up real estate, jacking up prices,
then abandoning the property as a tax write-off; receiving the corporate
welfare of government bail-outs and tax giveaways, loans and
grants—all the while paying minimal taxes; putting little or no significant money back into development and production and the creation of
jobs; upping the salaries of CEOs; and leaving the burden of paying for
the running of the country to middle and low-income workers.

Meanwhile, this was happening to the rest of us: thousands of jobs
were being eliminated or reduced in salary; agencies for temporary
workers became the major employers in the country; unions were virtually destroyed; houses became unaffordable and rents skyrocketed;
the number of homeless people increased on the streets; federal funds
to cities were drastically cut; more affluent white people moved to suburbs, leaving inner cities to the poor and people of color; human services

to both urban and rural people were either eliminated or cut, leaving low-income people to fend for themselves as best they could.

Number of U.S. corporations with $250 million or more in assets that paid no taxes:	1,555
Average size:	$1.2 billion in assets
Average sales:	$220 million per year
Percent of giant corporations that paid no taxes:	33.4%
Total federal taxes paid by these 1,555 giant corporations:	**$0.00**

GIANT CORPORATE TAX EVADERS
From: *Corporate Power and the American Dream*, The Labor Institute, NY, NY.

A great divide began forming. Not only did the globalization of the economy unleash corporate greed and irresponsibility, but other factors were at work. We are in the difficult transition from the industrial age to the technological, leading to more automation and fewer workers, and requiring highly trained, educated, and skilled workers. Class divisions are widening through the "professionalization" of the country, with the highly educated and skilled workers making livable incomes and those who have less education left to manual labor, the service industry, and temporary or part-time, low-skilled jobs—those remaining after the export of production to other countries for cheap labor. This transition carries with it as much disruption and displacement as the earlier transition from the agrarian age to the industrial.

Social disorder increased during the 1980s as the rich escaped social responsibilities, such as providing money for jobs and human services through re-investment of profits and payment of fair taxes, and instead opted for luxury spending that showed a concern only for selfish pleasures rather than the survival of all of us. The code of the times changed from one of responsibility, such as Harry Truman's "The buck stops here," to one of avarice that goes something like this: "Anything for a buck—the people and the environment be damned." Their bottom line seemed not to be "Is this good for the country?" but "Will this bring me more money?" Following that creed, television and movies produced

more and more violence because it was profitable, people were encouraged to run their credit cards up to the limit, and anything such as
affordable housing or day care that did not show a great profit was
abandoned. Workers' lives were destroyed as the rich eliminated their
jobs and lobbied for reduced taxes and regulation and less funding to
human needs programs. This pervasive immorality left the less affluent
in society to seek survival through dwindling jobs or the violence of the
streets. The loss of jobs and livable income broke up families, and communities were destabilized in the shifting economic struggles. By 1990,
it was obvious that something was terribly wrong in these United
States.

Clearly, for this system of unharnessed greed and affluence for the
few to continue, someone other than those responsible had to be
blamed. Otherwise we would see a rebellion, a people's revolt. Unjust
economic systems foster social chaos and require the imposition of
strong methods of control to keep order. Economic injustice requires
oppression to maintain social stability. When economic injustice and
oppression merge, it is difficult for people to rise up in a collective
response to bring about change.

THE MERGER OF ECONOMIC INJUSTICE AND OPPRESSION

During more than two decades of massive economic restructuring
and changes in class politics, progressive people have not managed to
keep a strong economic analysis in the public debate. Perhaps this failure has come from old fears derived from a history of red-baiting and
memories of the fairly recent McCarthy era of anti-Communism.
Certainly today, when progressive people point to the growing dispari-
ty between the rich and poor, conservatives immediately accuse us of
"trying to start a class war." Of course, the answer to this accusation is
that it is not progressives who began and perpetuate the ongoing warfare against the poor and middle classes of this country; it is those who
have redistributed wealth upward, leaving working people without adequate wages.

I have seen this warfare up close in over fifty years of living and
working in the South and traveling this country. People who discuss
economic injustice and suggest redistribution of wealth as a remedy are
inevitably labeled as neo-Marxists. Unfortunately, I am not schooled in

Marxism, only in capitalism as it was taught me in school and in the everyday life of this country, but my own lived experience has revealed injustice and made me long for economic fairness. The way I have learned to understand economics is as a value system; an analysis of a country's economic system and government budgeting reveals what it values most. Hence, it is not as an academic or an economist debating statistics and polls and studies that I present this discussion of the linkage of economics and oppression, but as a social and economic justice worker reporting what I have learned from my work.

First, some definitions:

Economic exploitation is using both people's labor and natural resources for the benefit of the few without adequate compensation for that labor or consideration of the environmental destruction created by the removal and disposal of those resources.

Oppression is the exertion of power and control over individuals and groups through discrimination, scapegoating, and violence, resulting in the denial of civil and human rights and the imposition of psychological violence.

For a long while the primary focus of progressive people has been the analysis of and remedies for oppression, and our failure to recognize its connection to exploitation has caused difficulty in both our analysis and in our organizing. For example, exploitation and oppression are almost always combined for people of color, but not always for other groups such as lesbians and gay men where oppression is pervasive but exploitation is intermittent. Thus, one of the most critical and damaging divisions we have among ourselves is along lines of class. Affluent white women are divided from low income women and women of color in the women's movement. Affluent white gay men and women are divided from low income lesbians and people of color in the lesbian and gay movement. These divisions have created our deepest fissures and led us to create incomplete politics based on oppression alone.

It is difficult for systematic economic injustice to be sustained without the backing of pervasive oppression. How does this work? One of the simplest ways I've found of explaining it is through a chart developed from an idea presented by Judith Stevenson to the steering committee of the NCADV in 1982. Since that time, Catlin Fullwood and I have expanded it in racism and homophobia workshops, and hundreds of other trainers and educators have used the "Power/Privilege Chart" to get people thinking and talking about the ways economic injustice and oppression work.

A Power/Privilege The Norm Dominator	B Less Power/Resources The Other Dominated
Rich	Poor
White	People of Color
Male	Female
Christian	Jews, Muslims, religious minorities
Heterosexual	Lesbian, gay, bisexual & transgender people
Able-bodied	People with disabilities

POWER/PRIVILEGE CHART

This chart is a reflection of the -isms of our times (classism, racism, sexism, anti-Semitism, homophobia/heterosexism, and ableism) and the struggle for equality and civil rights protections. Because most people have identities on both sides of the chart, it provides a door to understanding which people can walk through according to their experience of economic injustice and oppression, whether that be the experience of the dominator or the dominated. Probably the most important aspect of this chart is that in workshop and classroom discussions it requires participants to do critical thinking, the most important skill for the pursuit of freedom, equality, and justice, and the greatest enemy of authoritarianism. The compelling questions are "How does this work? How do those in column A manage to dominate those in column B?"

ECONOMICS

The most powerful factor on this chart is wealth, the top of column A. Some people argue that economic injustice and oppression occur because it is simply in people's nature to engage in the seven deadly sins of the Middle Ages: pride, gluttony, avarice, lust, sloth, anger, and envy. I and others, to the contrary, argue that economic injustice and oppression occur because someone benefits from them. It is in the interest of someone to create and perpetuate oppressions. The central question in any analysis of social/economic conditions is "Who benefits?" In almost every circumstance, those who dominate benefit from injustice, and those who benefit most are the rich.

When wealth resides in the hands of a few, rather than distributed throughout the population, then those few control the political, business, and social activities of a nation. Our government increasingly is one not of, by, and for the people, but of, by, and for the few. Despite Reagan's touting a "trickle down" theory of wealth, during the Reagan/Bush years the rich amassed greater wealth and the poor got poorer. In the 1990s, the structure of the U.S. economic holdings looks like a pyramid with a sharp narrow point on top. According to Holly Sklar in her extremely helpful book, *Chaos or Community?* (South End Press, Boston, 1995), "The combined wealth of the top 1 percent of American families is nearly the same as that of the entire bottom 95 percent....(They) owned more than half of all bonds, trusts and business equity; nearly half of all stocks; and 40 percent of non-home real estate in 1989. The bottom 90 percent owned about a tenth of all those assets, except non-home real estate, of which they owned 20 percent." Since 1989, that division has grown even wider and at an escalating rate. Wealth has not trickled down; it has been redistributed upward.

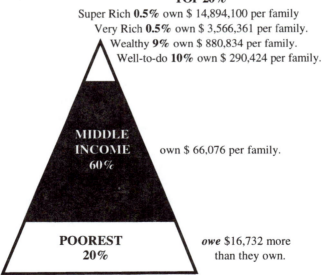

TOP 20%
Super Rich **0.5%** own $ 14,894,100 per family
Very Rich **0.5%** own $ 3,566,361 per family.
Wealthy **9%** own $ 880,834 per family.
Well-to-do **10%** own $ 290,424 per family.

MIDDLE
INCOME
60%   own $ 66,076 per family.

POOREST   *owe* $16,732 more
20%   than they own.

1989 AVERAGE U.S. NET WORTH
Source: Mishel & Bernstein, *State of Working America 1994-1995*,
M.E. Sharpe, 1994.

How do the few have so much while so many are scrabbling for so little? Certainly, the wealth of the rich comes not from the sweat of their brows and the work of their hands. Indeed, it is from the labor of others. For so much wealth to be accumulated in so few hands there must be an enormous source of *low-paid* and *unpaid* labor. In this country, that labor is produced by people of color, women, and minimally-educated white men, and in U.S. factories located in other countries, by large numbers of children as well.

A large portion of the unpaid labor which underpins this system is the volunteer work of women in the home and community. Without the free hours given by women we would have few charitable organizations in operation, our battered women's shelters would be closed, our churches and synagogues would be unable to function, our hospitals would be limited in care, programs for children would disappear, and families would not exist as we know them. These hours of volunteer time represent billions of dollars that need to be spent in meeting human needs. If meeting these needs were a high value in our budget priorities, salaries could be paid to these volunteer women for the support of themselves and their families. Everyone would benefit. Currently Congress is severely cutting all funding to support human needs in the name of balancing the budget, and like George Bush before them, the new Republicans are asking people to fill in the gap by volunteering. Volunteerism provides an inadequate buffer for the suffering caused when massive tax cuts that benefit the rich have forced human services to be reduced or eliminated.

An often unacknowledged source of unpaid labor is prisoners. In many states prisoners maintain highways, make license plates, etc., and constitute a portion of the unpaid labor pool. In other states such as Oregon, businesses, by law, can use them as unpaid/low-paid employees.

The lowest paid workers at the bottom of the pyramid are people of color and women (as well as white men with less than a high school education, teenagers, the old, and people with disabilities). They supply a bountiful source of low-paid labor. One-fifth of U.S. full-time workers are falling below the poverty level. (Sklar, p. 26) Despite the efforts of affirmative action programs, people of color and women still comprise the majority of low-income workers. Now Congress and the Supreme Court are at work dismantling affirmative action which has been this country's major attempt to give all people equal opportunity. Despite evidence to the contrary brought by the Reagan/Bush years, the prevailing theory remains that there is a level playing field and fairness will reign in a laissez-faire, free market system. Money, they insist, will trickle down from above to those below who do the work. But we ask: How much money? And is a trickle enough for people who are dying of thirst?

Let's look at how this trickle-down theory works for low-income people in this country by scanning the practices of one of the most popular discount chains, Wal-Mart. In 1989, according to *Forbes* magazine, Sam Walton, the founder of Wal-Mart, was the third richest man in the world, with $8.2 billion made from buying goods in enormous quantities and selling them to low and middle income people in small towns and in the working-class suburbs of large cities. Like other businessmen of his time, Sam sought goods that were cheaply made.

Decades ago, factories left the unionized North to settle in the South where "right to work" laws kept (and still keep) unions weak or nonexistent and salaries low. In more recent years, manufacturers found that people in Mexico or the Pacific Rim would work a whole day for what people in the South made in a minimum wage hour, so they moved their production to these countries. That's where Wal-Mart makes the cheap goods it brings back to the U.S. to sell to the working class—who are losing their jobs and their ability to consume because of the overall reduction of jobs and wages in this country. To appeal to these particular consumers, Wal-Mart instituted a "Made in America" campaign—however, the company was accused of buying goods that were made in other countries, where environmental and health laws were not in effect, and then brought into the U.S. for final assembly, where they got a label: "Made in the USA."

The practices of large discount stores affect the overall well-being of the community. Large numbers of women and people of color staff Wal-Mart stores. Many are hired on a less than full-time basis, now a common practice in businesses everywhere. Hence, no benefits, with the resulting higher profits going into Wal-Mart's coffers. Where huge Wal-Mart stores open, locally owned stores often close and small town centers disintegrate. The local shops cannot buy in such large quantities and offer competitive prices. The community is drastically changed when these small, locally owned businesses close down and business/civic cooperation is limited to arrangements with Wal-Mart.

In such common examples, the money does not trickle down but indeed is sucked upward. These practices explain a lot about the economic and social chaos of this country today. Mirroring the 1890s, billionaires such as Walton have become the robber barons of the late 20th century, exploiting people and the environment for the politics of greed and accumulation. Workers become dispensable and disposable, used and tossed away by corporations. However, they do not just disappear. Loss of jobs and income breed discontent. Workers and low-income people have to be repressed. Those who occupy the lower tier of the economic pyramid are yet to rise up to call for fairness in the relationship between wealth and those who labor to produce it. And that, I believe, is because they are held in place by greater forces than the need to make a decent living.

This economic system would not be able to work so successfully if there were not the oppressions of racism, sexism and classism, backed by institutions and the threat of violence, to hold people in place. Racism and sexism and classism are not simply social conditions; they are economic necessities of our times.

SCRABBLING FOR CRUMBS AT THE BOTTOM

Those who occupy the lower tiers of the economic pyramid are also pitted against one another for scarce jobs and resources. The Right rides high by fabricating the myth of scarcity—and the bottom 90% of the economic pyramid is held in place when people respond to this belief that there is not enough to go around. Here are the messages we are given: "There is not enough money, not enough good jobs, not enough civil rights, not enough quality education, not enough good health care, not enough grant money for non-profit organizations; there is just simply not enough to go around." (At the same time, we are told there *are* plenty of natural resources to go around, though we know this is not true because they are being consumed or destroyed internationally at alarming rates.) Yet, at the top 10% of the economic pyramid there is no scarcity of money or services or rights. In the June 1995 *Forbes* magazine, Bill Gates, head of the Microsoft Corporation, was named the world's richest person with holdings of $12.6 billion. David Sarasohn in *The Oregonian* (July 28, 1995) tells the story of how, after IBM had its best quarter ever, 120 executive secretaries were given salary cuts of up to 36% while IBM's top five executives split bonus money of $5.8 million—including a $2.6 million boost for CEO, Louis

Gerstner. Sarasohn goes on to cite the *Washington Monthly* (July/August 1995) as stating that in 1972, CEOs of the largest U.S. companies made 40 times their average workers' salaries, and now, in 1995, that figure is 140 times. There is not a scarcity of money in this country, it is simply held in too few hands.

Here's another false notion: if one receives something (from Medicare to civil rights protections) then someone else must lose—others are taking something from me. If economic inequity is to be maintained, it is critical that we believe there is not enough to go around and thus we must fight each other for a little piece of what's left, particularly along lines of race, gender, sexuality, and class. If welfare is provided for poor mothers and children, then there won't be enough money to pay the pittance of Social Security to the old. If women and people of color are brought into the workplace, then white men won't have jobs. If lesbians and gay men receive civil rights protections, then people of color will lose them. If undocumented immigrants are provided services, then citizens will lose money and services. If children receive bi-lingual or special education, then other children will receive inadequate education. The real problem is loss of jobs and the tax base for public services—and the concentration of enormous wealth and power in the hands of the few.

DIVERTING OUR ATTENTION FROM THE ECONOMY: THE RACIALIZATION OF ISSUES

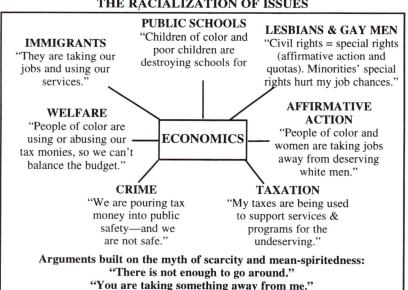

PUBLIC SCHOOLS
"Children of color and poor children are destroying schools for

IMMIGRANTS
"They are taking our jobs and using our services."

LESBIANS & GAY MEN
"Civil rights = special rights (affirmative action and quotas). Minorities' special rights hurt my job chances."

WELFARE
"People of color are using or abusing our tax monies, so we can't balance the budget."

ECONOMICS

AFFIRMATIVE ACTION
"People of color and women are taking jobs away from deserving white men."

CRIME
"We are pouring tax money into public safety—and we are not safe."

TAXATION
"My taxes are being used to support services & programs for the undeserving."

Arguments built on the myth of scarcity and mean-spiritedness:
"There is not enough to go around."
"You are taking something away from me."

We have long had the myth of scarcity, but what's new these days is the addition of mean-spiritedness: "There's not enough to go around—and *you* are taking something from me." These twin false-hoods provide the foundation for the current scapegoating that figures so strongly in ballot initiatives and the "hate" radio and television of people such as Rush Limbaugh.

We are led to believe that people who should be our natural allies are actually our enemies and we must compete with them for the little that trickles down. We are led to believe that we will succeed when we have fought each other hard enough to take our share of what is left over from the pie. The truth is denied; the pie was divided and distributed long before we even reached the table.

We are pitted against each other, both as identity groups and as individuals, for a small (and often temporary) piece of what should be our birthright: shelter, food, clothing, employment, health, education, safety, all dispensed with fairness and justice. Meanwhile, workers are robbed of jobs with livable wages and working conditions, women and children are violently abused, families deteriorate, people of color are marginalized in the social and economic life of the country, the environment becomes less life-sustaining every day, and great numbers experience the degradation of poverty.

The top 10% can go laughing to the bank, own one or more well-guarded and secured homes, send their children to prestigious schools, and take luxury vacations. There is no fairness or justice here.

INSTITUTIONAL SUPPORT FOR DOMINATION

Full domination requires the control of both institutions and the workplace, and the two intersect in the development of policy and laws. Those on the left-hand side of the Power/Privilege chart (rich, white, male, Christian, etc.) control both: financial institutions, government, religion, schools, human services, health care, criminal justice, as well as corporations, factories, and the majority of large businesses.

As an example, let's look at this country's major institution, the Congress. If we held up a photograph of the House and Senate, we would see that it is completely dominated by those from column A. Many are millionaires. There are very few poor people, people of color, women, Jews and Muslims, lesbians and gay men, people with disabilities. Is it because the they are not capable of serving, of making decisions that directly affect people like themselves? Certainly not, but it has everything to do with who can afford to run for office, who can fund their campaigns with a million or so dollars from personal wealth, or from other wealthy people and corporations and those who expect to gain from their tenure. It is virtually impossible for a poor person to be able to run for Congress, and consequently there are few people there who speak genuinely and from lived experience on behalf of the poor when laws and policies are made. Most of the people there speak on behalf of the interests that paid for them to be there. The Congress is probably the most important place for prohibiting or including the participation of those traditionally excluded and discriminated against, for if the members acted genuinely on behalf of their diverse constituencies, then the doors to justice and equality might open. (For this reason, the recent Congressional attempts to limit the right of nonprofits to lobby are particularly disturbing.)

It is the Congress, of course, that approves appointments to the U.S. Supreme Court, and state legislatures that have power over appointments to the supreme court of each state. State legislatures are more open to diverse membership but, like the U.S. Congress, tend to be dominated by wealthy white males, and they set our laws. Who benefits most from these laws? Again, those who occupy the left-hand side of the chart, but particularly the rich ruling class who provide financing for political campaigns and lobbying.

It is Congress and the courts that deal with laws and regulations affecting businesses and the control of the workplace. They can make regulations that protect workers' safety and health or remove them; protect the environment or allow it to be ravaged; provide access to collective bargaining or mandate "right to work" laws; raise the minimum wage, lower it, or eradicate it. But most importantly, they are in control of taxes; who gets taxed at what rate and how tax money gets spent. Or, how much from whom and for what. It is here that government bodies controlled by the rich serve the rich over and over again.

Again we ask, why don't those who experience injustice rise up? We don't because our domination is enforced with violence and the threat of violence. Congress, acting in concert with other branches of government, maintains social control through the criminalization of certain activities, through maintaining the police, the military, and intelligence gathering bodies, and also through what it permits to go unpunished. It oversees that institutional oxymoron, the criminal justice system. Certainly there was a chilling effect on those who rose up for justice in the Civil Rights Movement when police and dogs attacked people on the streets, when assassins killed its leaders, when the Klan was permitted to threaten and kill, and later, when police gunned down the Black Panthers. And there was a chilling effect on those who rose up to protest the war in Vietnam when the National Guard gunned down students at Kent State University in the 1970s.

As the fallout from corrupt policies creates worsening economic times and social disorder, legislative bodies respond by
- broadening the use of the death penalty,
- building so many prisons that, for many states, they become a source of major economic development,
- incarcerating large numbers of poor people,
- creating longer sentences and harsher prison conditions,
- increasing the number of police,
- eliminating prisoners' rights in prison and in the courts,
- increasing the number of border patrols,
- trying teenagers as adults,
- imprisoning greater numbers of women for charges such as hot checks or prostitution,
- and creating an overall prison population whose census is predominantly poor and disproportionately people of color.

There are also more pernicious forms of economic violence that keep people from rising up. Union activists report time and again that workers express a desire to join unions but have such a sense of overwhelming corporate dominance and threat of retaliation that they are afraid to act to change their circumstances. Additionally, continued economic deprivation can create need so intense that revolt is unthinkable.

So-called "justice" and money are intertwined. There is a clear message throughout the land: Poor people will be punished for crimes of property as well as passion; rich people can go free even after doing extraordinary harm to all of us through criminal acts such as the Savings and Loans and HUD debacles. In fact, not only will they go free after blatantly destroying our community life and the environment, but Congress will make the workers of this country pay to cover the consequences of the crimes of the rich—as evidenced by the Savings and Loan bailout.

At no time in recent history have we been more aware (and often simultaneously unaware) of the powers of Congress and legislative bodies, and it is here that we are observing the Right's revolution take place. We are witnessing a sweeping effort to eliminate taxes for the rich, to deregulate business, to privatize public lands and services, to eliminate the separation of church and state, to demolish the Bill of Rights for the sake of "law and order," to eliminate civil rights and civil liberties, to increase numbers of police, border patrols, and prisons, and to eradicate programs that attempt to equalize access to opportunity and to provide a safety net for basic human needs such as food, clothing, shelter, education, and safety. And all of this is being done by a group of people representing the interests of those who have power, wealth, and privilege, elected in 1994 by only the 36% of the electorate who bothered to vote.

Other significant institutions reflect the same domination. The health care industry, for example, is maintained by women and people of color; however, the upper 10% who make the decisions, reap profits and high salaries (doctors, administrators, boards, owners) are white men. It is not nurses, technicians, and line staff who are advocating for the development of HMOs and downsizing—eliminating their jobs, destroying their unions, or increasing their already overburdened jobs for less pay—it is the profit-makers within the medical profession and the insurance industry. Management wins; workers and patients lose. Consequently, this enormously rich high-tech country will not provide health care to all of its people because ordinary people cannot afford to pay the outrageously high rates which ensure large profit margins. Healing becomes subservient to profit; illness becomes a source of profit.

Institutions provide us with the information that shapes our lives, and controlling that information shapes how we think and live. We now consider ourselves to be an information society, with a highly developed mass media, electronic communication technologies, and a universal education system. Of those three, the media is probably the most influential, controlled by the businesses that buy advertising or provide the financial backing for movies and plays, television, radio, newspapers, books, and magazines. Because of corporate mergers, media ownership is concentrated in the hands of a few corporations; the theocratic Right owns the remainder. Media information, therefore, is determined by what is profitable to corporate owners or what serves right-wing ideology. Public broadcasting, the least controlled by business interests, is currently engaged in a life or death battle for survival in the face of right-wing attacks. Electronic communications are today the most accessible and probably most democratic, limited only by the cost of equipment and on-line time, but Congress is now acting on bills to censor and invade the privacy of these operations. Free speech and access to communication are critical because it is the media, especially television, along with schools that shape our thinking when we are young. In fact, our children are almost entirely enculturated by the media—which does not provide democratic access or discourse.

Schools provide a prime example of how our thinking is shaped. It is the common experience of people in the U.S. that those in affluent neighborhoods have good, well-funded schools, and those in poor neighborhoods get the leftovers. Schools serve corporate interests and are affected when those interests and needs change. In the mid-'80s, Arkansas Governor Bill Clinton convened the Business Council (locally known as the Good Suit Club), which was made up mostly of multi-millionaires, to provide guidance about the state's schools. At this time, Arkansas was ranked 48th in teacher salaries and 49th in per capita income but was listed in the 1988 *Forbes* 400 issue as having 12 multi-millionaires, more than anywhere other than the Upper East Side of New York City. Observing the Business Council, many progressive people wondered what interest chicken baron Don Tyson had in improving public education for his thousands of low-paid assembly line employees working in health-threatening conditions, cutting up chickens for market. They also wondered what interest Sam Walton had for improving the education of his low-paid workers who sell goods, made by even lower-paid workers in other countries, to low-income people in Wal-Mart discount stores in the U.S.

What we are learning is that with the U.S. expansion of capital and production into countries along the Pacific Rim and South America, both labor and the environment can be exploited with few restrictions, leaving corporations here with little need for large masses of educated workers. Instead, they require an educated elite providing management and a small corps of workers providing high electronic skills. Indeed, as corporations downsize, many highly educated and trained workers are being dismissed along with those who provide less skilled labor. Those jobs now most readily available to poor people—in the service industry and tourism—do not require much formal education. Capitalism, in its current international, unchecked movement, no longer needs public schools to provide a large, educated, skilled workforce.

Thus, in Little Rock, Arkansas, then-Governor Bill Clinton was asking men who are in the top one percent of the nation's wealthy to make decisions about public education.

It comes as no surprise that both rich and poor schools have curricula representing the people who control them. That is to say, the information children receive reflects the history, the literature, and the values of these people. It is a narrow, one-sided view of the world that reinforces the right of the dominators to dominate. The heroes children learn about are conquerors; the point of view of the conquered and the resisters is rarely presented. Those who lack power and privilege rarely read or hear anything from their point of view; they rarely encounter positive images of themselves. Domination is presented as a standard to aspire to; those who do not dominate or are dominated are seen as lacking and somehow wrong.

This system creates and sustains the idea that those who historically have had power and privilege are the *norm*. They are in control, in charge; the history they present shows they have always been and implies they always should be. Therefore they are right; in fact, they have earned the right to dominate throughout history. (Pat Buchanan, campaigning for the Republican presidential nomination, referred to himself and his followers as the "legitimate" descendants of "our founding fathers.") They are evidence of meritocracy at work. All others are to be judged by the norm; it is what we all should aspire to. Those who are not rich, white, Christian, heterosexual or able-bodied are the *other*. They are someone lesser, marginalized from the major decisions and the inner workings of society.

Institutions are the source of power for oppressions, reinforcing and perpetuating them daily.

THE TOOLS OF OPPRESSION

Those who exploit and oppress need ways to justify their actions. They need a rationale that shows they are in the right, that the majority both agrees and cooperates with them, and that people get what they deserve through their own merit or lack of merit. Economic and social injustice must become part of a framework of morality, complete with rewards and punishments, with exploitation and oppression entrenched. The superiority of the white race, of men, of Christians, of heterosexuals, of the rich becomes a given, a divine right to rule and dominate. The arguments go something like this: "We have always been in charge; therefore, it must be God's will. We won in the struggle for power; therefore, we must be virtuous. We were the framers of the Constitution and you were not included; therefore, it must belong to us."

But an ideology of entitlement is not enough. Those in power must get people to cooperate. People are not stupid, nor are we willing victims. Beyond the overt structures of economic and institutional control backed by violence and the threat of violence, there have to be more subtle and insidious social and cultural practices that bring us to act against our own best interest. In order for the privileged few to control the many, there have to be ways to divert attention from the root causes of social and economic problems; to focus instead on symptoms; to shift blame from the perpetrators to the targets of social and economic injustice—and to pit the latter against each other instead of against the perpetrators.

Here are some of those methods of diverting attention, shifting blame, and dividing people who should be allied with each other in the effort to end oppression.

• **Stereotyping**. Through stereotyping, groups of people (according to economic status, religion, gender, race, sexual identity, etc.) are thought of as one, and individual characteristics are overlooked or dismissed. In most cases, the negative behavior or characteristics of a few within the group, which may well be the result of institutionalized discrimination, are attributed to everyone in the group, and in some cases, negative qualities are simply fabricated. Also, qualities that go against the stereotype are overlooked—or those possessing them are called exceptions or are rewarded for being like the dominator, e.g., "she thinks like a man."

Some indicators of stereotyping are references to "*all* (women, Asians, disabled people, etc.)," "those people," "your people," "they." Any time people are lumped together in a group and generalizations made about them, we have stereotyping. Some examples:

"People on welfare are lazy and don't want to work. They abuse the system to make money. They don't appreciate nice things and simply ruin them when they are given anything nice. They are not good parents and don't take care of or control their children. They have babies just to get more money. They are almost all people of color."

"Jews are money-grubbing. They are loud, demanding, pushy. They control the media and financial institutions. They hate Christians.

They murder children. Jewish men are effeminate and unable to play sports. Jewish women are princesses."

"Lesbians and gay men recruit children because they can't have any. They sexually abuse children. They carry disease. They eat feces. Gay men act like women. Lesbians hate men because they have had a bad experience with them or they want to be men. They are perverted and militant. They all have sex in public."

"Blacks are lazy, unwilling to work. They want this country to give them something for nothing. They are oversexed. They have low morals and their children kill each other. They are not as intelligent as white people. They don't do well in schools or jobs. They hate whites. All they are good for is entertainment."

"Women are too emotional to be leaders; they get hysterical. They cannot do rational thinking and are weak in math and science. They use sex to get what they want and when they don't get it, they blame men. They are whores. They are manipulative. They are not strong enough to do physical work. They are tied to their biology. They gossip and are petty."

When commonly held, negative stereotypes become justification for harmful behavior and restrictive public policy toward people in each of the stereotyped groups. Thus the institution of slavery was not seen by white people as evil because Africans were said to be animals who did not have souls. For example, they supposedly did not feel the pain white people would feel when their children were wrenched away from them. Acts of injustice, such as the genocide of six million Jews, were interpreted as acts of social good because Jews were stereotyped as enemies of the Aryan nation. In the recent Texas case of a teenager accused of beating a gay man to death, he testified that he thought he had done society a service by eliminating a social evil. Accordingly, it is in the public good for Congress to eliminate Aid to Families with Dependent Children (what we know as welfare) to poor families because when they receive our tax dollars, they become lazy and avoid work. Individual and collective acts of violence become justified by both stereotyping and public policy.

• **Scapegoating**. While stereotyping is a matter of attitude, scapegoating is a matter of blame and works only when stereotyping is solidly in place in public thinking. Scapegoating is the process of shifting our attention away from the source of a problem and focusing it instead on another person or group of people. Jews, then, caused the economic problems in Hitler's Germany. Today, "abuses" of welfare by the poor cause the government's deficit spending. Lesbians and gay men cause the breakdown of the traditional family. Women having abortions cause the breakdown of the family and morality. African Americans and Latinos cause the breakdown of law and order in our cities. People of color and women benefiting from affirmative action cause loss of jobs for white men. Women in the workforce cause men to earn lower wages. Asian and Mexican immigrants cause job loss as well as the high cost of public services.

Scapegoating gives rise to violence and discrimination. It also fosters a lack of responsibility for seeking solutions to economic and social problems and for meeting human needs. For example, teenage mothers are currently blamed for straining welfare funds and contributing to the federal budget deficit. Efforts to eliminate welfare for teenage mothers (usually depicted as women of color) with one child suggest that because children are "illegitimate," we have no responsibility toward them.

In the worst of political times public policy is based on stereotyping and scapegoating. Efforts made to equalize opportunity and justice for all people get turned back. In local ballot initiatives, in state legislatures and Congress, and in the courts today we see new efforts to eliminate welfare, to destroy the tax base that provides public services, to eliminate affirmative action, to criminalize abortions, to resist civil rights protections for lesbians and gay men, to refuse to protect the rights of those accused of crimes, to eliminate free speech, to eliminate services to immigrants. And each action is justified by explanations of the harmful behavior of the targeted group, by those who think "these people" are not worthy of receiving the rights and privileges of living in a democracy.

For authoritarianism to take over, the general population has to be moved in broad emotional sweeps against scapegoated groups. Enemies of the people are created. Potential harms and losses are exaggerated. Division and fear are increased. It becomes in the "common good" to eliminate rights and to impose strict social control, enforced by the State through its police, FBI, CIA, and military. Quelling dissent and incarcerating large numbers of the population is mandated. And the people, out of fear and/or anger, must agree to give up much of their freedom in order to control others. When scapegoating is thoroughly effective and groups of people are perceived to be truly threatening, genocide can become the final solution.

• **Blaming the Victim**. While scapegoating is falsely holding a person or group responsible for the wrongs of others, blaming the victim occurs when the *targets* of an injustice are blamed for having caused the injustice. The groundwork for the blame is embedded in stereotyping. The perpetrator of the injustice did it to the victim because there was something wrong with her/him.

Nowhere do we see this false logic more clearly than in violence against women and children. "It's no wonder she was raped. What did she expect, being out on the street alone?" "I beat her because she would never get the meals on the table on time." "I had sex with my niece because she came on to me. What was I to do?" "I murdered her because I found her in bed with another man." "I hit her because she wouldn't stop talking." "When a woman dresses like that, she's asking for it." "The baby's crying was driving me crazy. So I beat him to shut him up." The perpetrator is absolved of responsibility for violence, and women and children come to believe there is something profoundly wrong with them. Even in our language we often shift the victim of violence from being the object of the attack to being the subject of the attack: "a wife was beaten by her husband" or "a black man was shot by the police" rather than "a husband beat his wife" or "the police shot a black man." This subtle shift in language diverts our attention away from the perpetrator.

Similar results occur in the workplace where we currently see workers blamed for the loss of jobs and income while attention is diverted from the practices of corporate management. "American workers aren't willing to work hard like those in other countries." "Workers' demands for raises have put us out of competition." "Organizing workers is a sign of disloyalty." "You haven't been willing to sacrifice to keep this company going." "You are lazy, pampered, and spoiled." "You are too old and outdated to be competitive." While workers are being turned against each other, there is no collective action to hold management accountable for choosing to compete in global markets by cutting labor costs, and for overworking and underpaying employees (those who remain after downsizing) in order to keep productivity and profits high.

Placing the blame for racial injustice on its victim is traditional in this country. "The Indians were savages. We had to fight and kill them to develop this country." "We hired one (African American, Asian, etc.), but she didn't work out." "If black people would stop killing each other, then the police wouldn't be so rough on them." "We want to hire more people of color, but there just aren't any qualified applicants." "Generations of welfare and innate laziness have made them unwilling to work." "Their genetic make-up makes them inclined to crime and poverty." The current effort to racialize our social and economic problems is filled with blame for those who most often experience the destructive effects of these problems.

Dehumanization and, often, demonization allow the perpetrator(s) to justify the oppression and destruction of human beings. Blaming the victim for injustice against him/her absolves the perpetrator of responsibility, and it combines neatly with stereotyping and scapegoating. Stereotyping, scapegoating, and blaming the victim flourish in the absence of critical thinking and in the presence of rising systemic injustice.

THE EFFECT OF SYSTEMIC OPPRESSION

Stereotyping, scapegoating, and blaming the victim make targeted groups feel there is something wrong with us individually and as identity groups (such as women), rob us of our sense of self and our respect for others, and prevent us from supporting and joining others. However, it is also in this area of individual and group self-worth, responsibility and accountability that we have the most control, the most ability to make change, the most hope for resistance.

• **Internalized Oppression**. Internalized oppression requires a book unto itself. It is a profound, complex issue that has attracted much study and can be treated only in a cursory manner here. It is absolutely central to the concerns of people who want whole self-fulfilling lives for themselves and their communities. Freedom from internalized oppression—receiving the negative messages of society and internalizing them as self-hating, self-blaming, self-policing—is directly linked to liberation. Many of us now recognize that we cannot build a liberation movement with people who have diminished hope, pride and belief in themselves.

Internalized oppression is more than low self-esteem, which implies an individualized mental health issue calling for an individualized therapeutic solution. Whereas low self-esteem can be caused by injurious *individual* treatment, internalized oppression originates from

33

pervasive negative cultural messages and mistreatment toward a person because of who s/he is *as part of a group* (women, people of color, lesbians and gay men, people with disabilities) within the larger context of society. The elimination of internalized oppression calls for group action on behalf of oneself and one's people.

The damaging effect of stereotyping, blaming the victim, and scapegoating is not only that the general public accepts such negative beliefs, but that the targets of these beliefs also come to accept that there is something wrong with themselves and their people. Not only does the dominant culture absorb these cultural messages, we all do. Hence, it is not surprising that a black child would choose white dolls over black ones or think that his/her friends were never going to be successful—or to think that the best of the black community are light-skinned. Or that lesbians and gay men would worry about being abnormal, or about going to hell for who we are—or would choose invisibility and try to pass as heterosexuals. Or that Jews would "fix" their noses, take on anglicized names or make efforts to pass as Gentiles. We have received strong messages that it is dangerous to be like our own people and therefore different from the norm.

It is also very difficult to be true to ourselves and our uniqueness when the ways we are different from the dominant culture have been labeled as deviant, disgusting, and dangerous. When literature, history books, art, movies, and television show a multi-faceted, positive vision of the dominators and a single, negative vision of the dominated, then a person growing up female, of color, lesbian or gay, etc., has to work against the entire culture in order to develop a sense of pride and wholeness. Most of the images shown us come directly from negative stereotyping.

All our major liberation movements have had a cultural component that builds group pride and demonstrates the diversity of our community attributes. It is an effort to counter stereotyping by presenting the broad range of our differences and achievements. "Black is beautiful" was a theme that ran through the later days of the Civil Rights Movement and was the bedrock of the Black liberation movement; black women and men wore natural hairstyles; African inspired clothing gained popularity; children were provided black dolls and books with black heroes. The Lesbian/Gay/Bisexual/Transgender Movement celebrates a "pride" day each year with parades, rallies, banners, and all the trappings of lesbian and gay culture. The Women's Movement has lifted up women's culture, unearthing women's history, writing books about women's lives and experiences, creating conferences and festivals, women's music, and women's sports. Perhaps its most powerful contribution to the elimination of internalized sexism was the consciousness-raising groups of the early 1970s which gave women an opportunity to talk about the negative messages and social conditioning we had received and to take action together for change.

This is what we must be ever mindful of: to create self-hatred and low self-esteem in a people is to weaken their will for survival. It is then a more simple task to dominate them, free of the threat of organized resistance. In order to resist, we have to believe that we are worthy, our lives are worthy, and our people are worthy enough for us to live and die for in the struggle for freedom, equality, and justice.

• **Horizontal Hostility**. Internalized oppression and horizontal hostility are closely connected. When we think of ourselves and our people as lacking in value—as being inferior and incapable, as being at fault for our lack of equality—then we begin to hold contempt for one another. That contempt is a reflection of the contempt we have been taught to feel for ourselves and people like us. To strike out at our own kind is to exhibit not only rage and frustration but also despair. Internal community or organizational conflict creates alienation and separateness, and the destruction of hope for working together to make change.

Rather than working together, we strike out against one another instead of against those who control our lives. For many of us, the pain we feel at the hands of our own people (family, friends, neighbors, allies) is far worse than what we feel from the more distant and abstract institutions and forces that harm our lives in dreadful ways every day. It happens in the arena where we care the most—in our daily lives—and with the people closest to us. This is also the place where we feel the most power for fighting back.

Some of our communities are devastated by our violence against each other on the street. Some of our organizations are racked with virulent infighting. We destroy our leaders. We hear statements such as "I'd rather work for a white man any day than for (a woman, a black person, etc.)." We attack each other in the street, in the office, in our organizations, in the press. We falsely identify our enemy as the person next to us (who actually shares the same oppression or exploitation) currently causing us a problem rather than the larger forces (often unseen) that control our overall well-being. We then turn our anger and outrage at our own people, holding them responsible for all the injustice we have experienced. The true cause of our injustice is overlooked or excused.

Many times I've been in meetings to create strategies for social change and had those meetings break down into interpersonal conflict, struggles for power, accusations of oppressive (sexist or racist, for example) behavior—with people left feeling hopeless because there was so much pain and so few possibilities for resolving conflict and healing wounds. Everyone's history of pain and injustice had been brought to the table, seeking either balm or retribution. Disappointment led to destructive behavior.

Horizontal hostility takes the heart out of us. It strikes where we care the most. Nothing could make the dominators happier; we do their business for them by holding each other down, and they don't have to lift a hand.

• **Identification with Power**. We make the politics of domination work by believing in and identifying with those in power rather than with our natural allies—those who also experience inequality and injustice—and also when we dream of having the power to dominate. If we feel a loss of power in certain areas of our life—because we are gay, or female, or a person of color—then we often identify with and try to take our power from the area of our life that is recognized as powerful. Thus, for example, we can find some gay white males acting out the privilege they gain from being white and male and not identifying with women and people of color. Organizationally, we see them holding power over and often excluding lesbians and people of color and refusing to take on issues that would threaten white, male, or class dominance. Or, in some cases, a poor, black woman will take her privilege from her heterosexuality and work against the inclusion of lesbians and gay men in civil rights protections. In the workplace we see workers sometimes identifying their interests with the boss rather than the unionists. In the end, the failure of people to identify with other oppressed groups means that they prevent the possibility of gaining freedom in the areas where they themselves are oppressed. They participate in the same structure of domination that holds them down.

This identification with power interests is evident in many of our organizations that work for social and economic justice. We have internal divisions because we have not overcome our racism, sexism, homophobia, classism. For instance, in a women's organization, one might find that the group agrees upon issues concerning sexism but is racked with racism, classism and homophobia, thus alienating the women of color, lesbians and poor women in its constituency. Power is taken from the place where they are dominant—as white, middle-class heterosexuals. When organizations have not recognized and worked internally upon the presence of related oppressions, they are often inclined to fight for turf for their own single interest in coalition work with other identity groups. They subscribe to the belief in a hierarchy of oppressions, wherein not only are some oppressions seen as more important than others, but some are seen as more deserving of attention and resources. Divisive competition rather than cooperation occurs.

This is where the Right has had phenomenal success in moving us to act against our best interests. They have carefully crafted messages that say, "Someone is trying to horn in on the one area where you (an individual, organization, or community) have been successful: that very place where you experience what little power you have." In African American communities, these messages say, "Lesbians and gay men are trying to hijack the Civil Rights Movement; they are also an affront to your Christianity." Among retirees they say, "Your real estate tax dollars are being spent wastefully on schools and social services you no longer even require because you have no children at home." Among working-class white men they say, "Women and people of color are taking your jobs, and despite your hard work, the demands of unions have forced us to close down our factories and move." When fighting each other we fail to see the complex causes of the injury and injustice we experience.

• **Individual Solutions**. Identifying with and joining our natural allies in pursuit of justice would create a strong and unified movement. It is therefore critical to the dominators that we be separated from one another and not recognize our common interests. Rather than identifying with those from whom group power is withheld, people often identify with those who guard the gates because there is the promise of a taste of power for the "deserving" few. The system is held in place by the idea that a few people can cross over or rise up if they try hard enough, are smart, and if they take on the values of those in power. Competition and rivalry between striving individuals or groups will pay off. Individual merit will bring the best to the top. This is the American Dream: the notion that one can be the exception to the rule and, by hard work and good luck, can join the few at the top. It is the carrot that draws many people onward.

The idea that only individual effort counts makes us believe that if we only please the dominator, then our lives will improve. That is, if we assimilate (drop our cultural differences and beliefs), we will be accepted into the realm of power: A tough "dress-for-success" woman will get a job equal to a man's; a Clarence Thomas who opposes civil rights will get a place on the Supreme Court; the passing gay man will be a sports star; the low-paid worker who does not join the union can become a manager. For these achievements in tokenism, one is asked to identify with the dominator, not the community. Sometimes people rationalize that, once they get a footing, they individually can change the institution or business from the inside. What they often fail to recognize is that, in their unsupported battle, they are receiving power that is conditionally *given*, not power that is *won* through the struggles of people for equality and justice. What is given can as easily be taken away. Individual ambition and reward are mistaken for social change.

An example of the tension between individual and group efforts can be found within the women's anti-violence movement. In its early years, many of its workers and leaders were survivors of violence and their work was directed toward helping women heal through group discussion and finding ways to change the system that allows violence against women to continue. When women's anti-violence organizations began to achieve community credibility in the 1980s, "professionals" sought jobs within them, and the work increasingly focused on delivery of services to individual women and on healing through individual therapy. Much of the focus on collective action and systemic change was lost.

This idea of individual effort and individual solutions can be a major block to building a liberation movement. Of course, individual effort is a good thing, and we want an appropriately balanced combination of individual and group effort. However, if people see all problems as individual and the solutions contingent upon the success or failure of individual efforts, then there cannot be collective organizing. An emphasis on individual effort alone ignores structures of oppression and leaves them intact. We then fail to recognize that there is a conscious and deliberate system of oppression and exploitation affecting the economy and social welfare of our people—and that it is a system that can be changed.

THE RIGHT AND THEIR AGENDA

The Right consists of individuals and groups that range from conservative, free-market capitalists to white supremacist neo-Nazis. It is not monolithic but a confederacy of loosely related individuals, groups, and organizations, some of which work in coalition with each other, some of which simply work toward similar goals, and some of which oppose each other. They do not act in a vast conspiracy, but their work often complements and supports each other to advance the effort to control the economic and cultural climate. In this discussion, except for references to specific ideological groups such as the theocratic Right, "the Right" will refer to this confederacy of groups that promotes an agenda that limits access to social and economic equality and justice.

The Right has a long history in this country, stronger in some periods of time, less so in others. It tends to be the most visible and active after people's victories in their efforts to achieve equality. For instance, the Right was particularly active after the abolition of slavery, using racial discrimination and segregation in the form of Jim Crow laws and the terrorism of the Klan to create a climate of fear. After the successful growth of labor unions and the victories of World War II over fascism, the Right organized virulently around anti-Communism and was particularly visible in the McCarthy and House Un-American Activities Committee hearings. More recently, we have seen the Right grow in strength since the passage of the Civil Rights Act of 1964, organizing around economic and social issues that limit access to democratic processes and the workplace. Attacking people on the basis of race, gender, sexuality, and economic class always has been a central strategy of right-wing organizing to build new antagonisms and exploit pre-existing divisions, and to organize in defense of privilege for white people, men, and the wealthy. Since the 1960s, the economic chaos caused by reduction in jobs and wages as corporations entered global markets has created particularly fertile ground for the growth of the Right.

• MAJOR MOVEMENTS •

LIBERATION MOVEMENTS (Civil Rights, Women's, Lesbian/Gay, People with Disabilities)	GLOBALIZATION OF THE ECONOMY	RISE OF RELIGIOUS RIGHT-WING FUNDAMENTALISM
Demand for full participation	Decision to keep profits high by reducing labor costs	Reactionary response to economic and social unrest

Strategies (Liberation Movements):
- Ignite conscience of nation through civil disobedience to recognize and end discrimination
- Gain entry into education & the workplace
- Redefine & expand gender roles
- War on Poverty
- Break silence on sexual & physical abuse of women & children
- Expand definition of the family
- Establish reproductive choice

Strategies (Globalization of the Economy):
- Downsize businesses
- Deregulation
- Weaken unions
- Reduce salaries
- Increase productivity by raising hours worked
- Use part-time & contingent workers
- Automate production
- Move production to cheaper labor markets
- Lobby for increased tax breaks
- Privatize public lands
- Redistribute wealth upwards

Strategies (Rise of Religious Right-Wing Fundamentalism)
- Foster cultural war against gains of liberation movements
- Dismantle civil rights & liberties
- Scapegoat poor & people of color to divert attention from real cause
- Racialize issues to pave way for authoritarian rule
- Organize men to assert hierarchy of domination
- Mobilize heterosexuals to oppose civil rights protections

Issues (Liberation Movements):
- Reproductive rights
- Abortion
- Affirmative Action
- Busing
- Head Start
- Title VII
- Children's rights
- End hate violence
- Women's anti-violence
- ERA
- Repeal sodomy laws
- End environmental racism

Issues (Globalization of the Economy):
- Anti-tax
- Deregulation
- Wise Use
- Anti-Union
- NAFTA
- Privatization
- Public vote on tax increases
- Litigation reform (restrict ability to sue companies)

Issues (Rise of Religious Right-Wing Fundamentalism):
- Abortion
- School Prayer
- Homosexuality
- Censorship
- Traditional family values
- Privatization of public schools/services
- Teenage pregnancy
- Immigration
- Crime
- Drugs
- Welfare

Motivation
Liberation/Inclusion

Motivation
Self-interest

Motivation
Fundamentalist, God-inspired hierarchy

Goal
A multiracial, multicultural, participatory democracy

Goal
Redistribution of wealth upward

Goal
Merger of church and state

Result
Increased participation

Result
Economic and social chaos

Result
Theocracy based on authoritarianism

It is difficult to keep track of the interconnectedness of the different groups, particularly the role business conservatism and global corporate capitalism play in the advancement of the policies of the Right. In the past three decades we have witnessed massive changes in the globalization of the economy and in the radical redistribution of wealth from the middle and working classes into the hands of the top 10% of the population. Corporate leaders in general have embraced and benefited from many of the policies of the Right. Not only have they supported the Right's institutions such as the Heritage Foundation with major financial contributions, but they have become involved in the efforts to erode the tax base for public services and to deliver public lands over to private ownership and corporate development.

A more elusive connection is between corporate managers and the theocratic Right. Those who have wreaked economic havoc through downsizing and eliminating jobs for workers—from the lowest paid to middle managers—need some way to stabilize the ensuing economic and social chaos. The theocratic Right positions itself to be in charge of the clean-up operation, proposing to bring order to this chaos by providing an authoritarian vision and by diverting our attention away from corporate greed to instead focus scorn and indignation on groups struggling for inclusion as equal participants in society. Corporations are protected; people are blamed; communities fall apart. This unsettled climate of social and economic distress and confusion gives the theocratic Right the perfect opening to develop their agenda of authoritarian control. In return, conservative business interests serve the theocratic Right well by working for privatization, clearing the way for church-dominated (formerly public) institutions.

The roles of the white supremacists and neo-Nazis are somewhat more obvious. They are the defining far right edge of an often violent, racist, anti-Semitic agenda, and people such as David Duke and Patrick Buchanan help keep white supremacy in the public debate. The far Right creates a magnetic draw for the center of the political spectrum to move further right because of its appeal to historic and current racism.

Perhaps it is easier to identify and understand the theocratic Right as a coalition of religious conservatives, many of whom are fundamentalists, who are working to create a government run by officials who claim divine authority from a Christian god.

In the 1960s, religious fundamentalism began to increase around the world. The theocratic Right began to be recognized as a contemporary phenomenon in the U.S. in the 1970s, when its leaders were recruited by New Right leaders who had organized from the campaign of Barry Goldwater. Those leaders were conservative strategists who were shaping a racist backlash to the Civil Rights Movement, especially its key elements of affirmative action and busing. The theocratic Right could move masses of people because it could strategically exploit people's religious faith to advance their right-wing secular political agenda. This vital arm of the Right focused its strategy on cultural issues such as sexuality and gender (i.e., homosexuality, abortion, feminism) and less overtly on race. Beginning in the early 1970s, for example, as the public school system was struggling to meet the challenges of racial integration, the theocratic Right launched a series of campaigns against "secular humanism" and sex education curricula, and in favor of prayer in the schools and "school choice." The theocratic Right generated a network of private religious schools, many of them all-white. By the 1990s, the growing racialization of issues such as crime, welfare, immigration, and affirmative action enabled the Right to mobilize white people to support its anti-democratic agenda. Also effective was the covert use of sexism (exemplified by the Promise Keepers) to organize men to assert hierarchical domination, and homophobia to organize heterosexuals to redefine and dismantle civil rights and liberties.

Both thrusts—the overtly racist Right and the theocratic Right—have created scapegoats for national social and economic problems as America's standard of living declines and its tax base is eroded by government giveaways to Fortune 500 companies in the form of massive tax breaks. By propagating vehement anti-Communism and anti-liberalism as well as exploiting the backlash against the Civil Rights Movement, the Right managed to divert our attention away from an unprecedented redistribution of wealth in the 1970s and 1980s that made the wealthiest even richer and dramatically reduced the standard of living for working people.

Because their views are highly visible through their own media outlets and through the coverage of the corporate media, and because of the success of their grassroots organizing, the theocratic Right is the right wing's most visible face to the general public. During this time of social and economic crisis, they build wide support by appealing to people's fears. They urge us all to support social and political exclusion of those different from ourselves. By mobilizing to change institutions and government, they seek to limit who gets to be full working partners in the everyday life of this country and who gets to have full access to food, clothing, shelter, safety, and health.

Some of their dominant organizations and leaders are the Christian Coalition (Pat Robertson), Focus on the Family (James Dobson), Traditional Values Coalition (Lou Sheldon), American Family Association (Donald Wildmon), Concerned Women for America (Beverly LaHaye), Eagle Forum (Phyllis Schlafly), and Operation Rescue (Randall Terry). On the local level, there are organizations that are affiliated with these national groups. For instance, in Oregon their primary organization is the Oregon Citizens Alliance (Lon Mabon) which has developed groups in Washington and Idaho in a strategy for dominance in the Northwest.

The Right is supported by numerous well-funded institutions: policy think tanks such as the Heritage Foundation, legal arms such as the Rutherford Institute and the American Center for Law and Justice, political organizing groups such as Focus on the Family, and media outlets such as the Christian Broadcasting Network.

In all of this, it is important to remember that there is significant difference between the leaders of the Right, particularly the theocratic Right, and their followers. Whereas the leaders have a clear agenda of domination and use tactics that are often manipulative, cynical, and dishonest, their followers quite often are lower and middle-class working people who are alarmed by the losses they have suffered in the economy over the past two decades, and they are desperately seeking solutions to the problems they experience. Many of them are Christians whose heartfelt faith has been exploited for the secular purposes of a right-wing political agenda. They should not be dehumanized or abandoned as potential allies in the struggle to defend democracy and diversity.

THE RIGHT'S GOALS

An examination of the Right's activities and public statements indicates their goals are to

• establish more rigid social control through reinforcing traditional hierarchical structures and increasing the police arm of the state;

• redefine and dismantle civil rights;

• promote unequal social and economic opportunity based on individual merit and privilege gained from belonging to the historically dominant class, race, gender, and religion;

• eliminate barriers to an unregulated free market.

The success of the collective forces of the Right is enhanced by the fact that the theocratic Right embraces these goals (adding their own framework of goals to the mix) and works on every level, from the small local church to the Supreme Court, to achieve their right-wing agenda through grassroots organizing, direct action, media, legal, and electoral strategies.

The broad goal of the theocratic Right is to replace democracy with theocracy, merging church and state so that authoritarian (and male) leaders enforce a fundamentalist vision in this country's public and private life. This goal is illustrated in these comments of the Christian Coalition's Pat Robertson: "I believe that [Jesus] is lord of the government, and the church and business and education, and, hopefully, one day, lord of the press." (*Christianity Today*, 6/22/92).

The theocratic Right's vision, developed from a narrow and literal interpretation of the Bible, is of a white God who gives authority directly to man to have power and dominion over the earth, its people, and its material resources. The belief in this hierarchy supports the domination of women, people of color, and nature by white men. The theocratic Right, white supremacist Right, and corporate Right all act in their narrow self-interest, and not in the interest of a majority of people or of social justice or of democracy. Any strides by oppressed groups toward autonomy and independence and full participation in society threaten this hierarchy. The theocratic Right acts as the ground troops of the collective forces of the Right and works to dismantle the gains of the Civil Rights Movement for people of color and women, vehemently opposes reproductive rights, tries to prevent lesbians and gay men from achieving equality, and opposes efforts to protect the environment. The work is done in the name of morality, law and order, and free-market capitalism.

THEIR TARGETS

In the past two decades, the Right has vigorously opposed teaching evolution, multi-culturalism and sex education, school-based clinics, HIV/AIDS education, gay and lesbian equality, welfare, parental leave, tax increases for public funding of entitlements and social services, environmental protections, reproductive rights, battered women's shelters, the Equal Rights Amendment, the United Nations, the National

Endowment for the Arts, the Corporation for Public Broadcasting, the Department of Education, affirmative action, pay equity for women, immigrants, and union organizing.

They have supported creationism, laws to increase the rights of private property owners, home schooling, school vouchers, censorship of books and the arts, anti-environmental laws, fathers' rights, states' rights, laws limiting protection for victims of abuse, strict crime and punishment and prison reform laws, expansion of the death penalty, privatization of social programs, severe immigration laws, "right to work" and other laws designed to destroy unions, English-only laws and other anti-immigrant proposals, and laws requiring that tax increases be limited and submitted to the public vote for approval.

In all that they oppose or support, it is people of color, women, children, lesbians and gay men, poor people, and the environment that will suffer most if they succeed in their goals. In the end, it is all of us because the repression of these targeted groups of people will limit the lives of everyone in the U.S. When, for example, the tax base that funds public services is destroyed, everyone will suffer from the reduction in the number of public schools and public libraries that help create a universally literate populace and a rich culture. If public safety is given over to private companies who serve people living in gated suburbs, then those suburban homes will become their own kind of prisons behind walls and gates. When the environment is poisoned, everyone will have to breathe polluted air, not just poor people. And in a Christian theocracy, there would be little freedom for Jews, Hindus, Muslims, and persons with other spiritual and secular philosophies and beliefs.

THEIR STRATEGIES

The Right hopes to accomplish its anti-democratic goals by casting a wide net of governmental, corporate, legislative, cultural and social strategies that destroy the possibility of equal participation in this country's public and economic life.

One must always remember that *misinformation* is a primary tactic in all that they do; that at the center of their organizing message on each issue is a heightened sense of scarcity, "There's not enough to go around," combined with mean-spiritedness, "You are taking something from me," with a focus on people of color as the primary problem; and that they move so quickly—as witness the Republican-dominated 104th Congress—their strategies are changing rapidly even as I write about them. Some examples of tactics the Right uses and some possible results if they are successful:

• **Taxation**. This is perhaps the core issue. Increasingly, throughout the country there are anti-tax measures on ballots and in Congress that would eliminate historic sources of taxes such as property or corporate tax. Generally, the ballot measures reduce existing taxes, put a cap on future taxes, and require that all tax increases be put to the public vote, requiring a two-thirds majority to approve them. These cuts most adversely affect the lower and middle classes and benefit the wealthy. Additionally, massive tax breaks through other tax legislation (often written by corporate lobbyists) are given to corporations. While the federal deficit has grown out of control, corporate taxes have dropped about 40% since the 1970's, costing the government a loss of $700 billion in revenue. (*Dollars and Sense*, Sept/Oct 1995, p. 35)

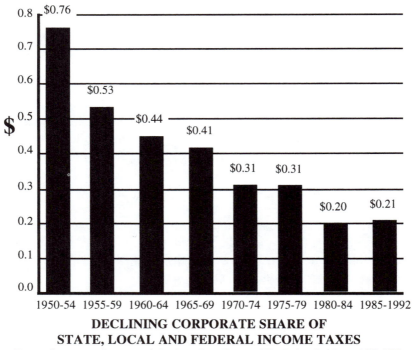

**DECLINING CORPORATE SHARE OF
STATE, LOCAL AND FEDERAL INCOME TAXES**
From: *Corporate Power and the American Dream*, The Labor Institute, NY, NY.

Because the outcome of elections is generally heavily influenced today by the amount of media exposure groups can purchase, the anti-tax initiatives (with the financial backing of major corporations) are often successful. Massive media campaigns can effectively sway the general public which is frightened by current economic conditions and generally mis- or uninformed about tax policy. By planting and then repeating the idea of scarcity and loss, the Right has been able to bring together a very politically diverse group of people and introduce them to a piece of their anti-democratic agenda. Using economic fears and scapegoating, the Right organizes working people against welfare recipients, native-born citizens against immigrants, white men against women and people of color.

Result: The tax base is weakened until there are inadequate public funds to pay for basic services such as police, fire departments, schools, libraries, and social programs. These services are eliminated or become privatized and fall into the control of corporate America or religious institutions. In California, the premier tax revolt initiative, Proposition 13, which imposed tax limits has led to large government deficits and near disaster in state and local services. For instance, in Merced County, officials announced in November 1993 that to save a needed $1.4 million a year, all 19 of its public libraries would have to close in 1994. (Richard Reeves, *Money*, Jan 1994, p. 93) James Sterngold, writing about the effect of Proposition 13 in California, notes that education has undergone a slow but dramatic decline there. In the mid-1960s, California had the fifth-highest expenditure rate per pupil in the country and an envied education system. Today it is 42nd in spending, has one of the highest dropout rates in the country—only two are worse—and last year fourth-graders in California tied for last place in an educational assessment test given in 39 states. (*New York Times* News Service, Aug 6, 1995).

Of equal concern is the idea that if public institutions are privatized, then they cannot be held accountable to the general population for their policies and practices. Community boards and avenues for public input and influence can be eliminated. Many people are drawn to support privatization because they believe that if institutions are operated as businesses, they will be more cost efficient, but the savings often come from a reduction in services or standards, e.g., if services for sexually abused children cost too much, then savings can be made by reducing the standards for reporting.

Eliminating taxes for public services is perhaps the most devastating of all the strategies of the Right because lack of funds causes the basic infrastructure of the country to crumble, leaving services (when available) only for those who can purchase them. It calls the fundamental democratic question of the responsibility of the individual to the collective and vice versa. A basic tenet of a pluralistic, democratic society is the interplay of individual freedom and mutual responsibility. An indicator of societal dissolution is the loss of mutual responsibility. The destruction of the financial infrastructure sets the course for scapegoating welfare recipients and immigrants as primary causes of our economic problems.

Voting by a two-thirds majority on every tax and fee increase basically ensures defeat and hamstrings government in fulfilling its duties to the general population. It is the anti-tax movement that can render government incapable of functioning and of being able to reduce the deficit in any significant way.

• **Workers' Rights and Unions**. Working people organizing collectively in unions have struggled successfully for the 8-hour day, child-labor laws, public education, unemployment insurance, social security, medical and health benefits, paid sick leave, health and safety laws, and the minimum wage—changes that benefit both organized and unorganized workers. Union wages and benefits are a benchmark for unorganized workers. Despite these successes (or more likely because of them) unions have been under intensified attack by the Right since capital began global expansion. In the 1980s, the policies of the Reagan/Bush administration became the blueprint for weakening and destroying unions.

Reagan's handling of the PATCO (air traffic controller) strike in 1981 signaled open season on historically protected rights for workers to act collectively. His authorization to terminate the strikers and replace them with permanent replacement workers marked a dramatic shift toward protecting business against workers. That was followed by Reagan's underfunding and understaffing (or staffing with people hostile to workers) the National Labor Relations Board, the Department of Labor's Occupational Safety and Health Administration, and the Equal Employment Opportunity Commission.

These policies continue in the 1990s, with some additional twists. In the effort to render government incapable of protecting the interests of the poor, people of color, women, and workers, the Right has engaged in an overt strategy of destroying the tax base, deregulating businesses, and fomenting anti-government sentiment. Public employees, many of whom are organized into unions and many of whom are people of color, have a history of organizing against these efforts. The Right has named them the "new elite," and is scapegoating them as the culprits of what is wrong with the government. Unions are a major target of both corporations and the Right because they are the primary voice speaking against the current unjust economic policies, and they are the only institution that has a strong organizing structure capable of mobilizing large numbers of people. Unfortunately, unions have become even more vulnerable because they have lost the strong support of the Democratic party. Democrats, having moved gradually to the right over the last decade, have reduced their historic support for labor and increasingly embraced business interests.

Result: In a time of rising power of the Right, labor is weakened, factionalized, and faced with erosion of legal protection for workers to organize. While labor's history has not always been perfect, it has been the representative of working people when their interests needed to be advanced, in the form of electoral campaigns of pro-worker legislators, through the initiative process, through education and research, or through the capacity to organize resistance to the Right. The anti-union policies of the Reagan/Bush administration resulted in the gutting of agencies and laws protecting workers' rights so that unions became hamstrung in their ability to represent their members. In this time when working people are under harsh attack, their jobs and salaries eroding and working conditions worsening, any hope of successful opposition lies in the ability of people to come together and organize resistance. Now, however, workers are being organized against workers as the successes unions have won for their members become labeled the cause of the economic woes of unorganized workers. If the Right succeeds in destroying the ability of workers to organize effectively for power, working people will be forced to accept whatever terms their bosses offer them in a rapidly changing climate in which they are increasingly abused or abandoned for greater profits in a globalized economy. Without unions, working people are left without a means of working collectively for economic justice.

• **Lesbians and Gay Men.** The issue of homosexuality has provided a major source of fundraising for the Right's organizations as well as their best vehicle for changing the country's thinking about civil rights. For several years, homosexuality has been the flash point of the theocratic Right's organizing; they have mounted an extraordinary campaign of distortion to play on the public's economic and social fears and to prepare the way for their larger goal of eroding civil rights protections for people of color and women. Demonizing lesbians and gay men as disease-carrying sexual predators whose purpose is to destroy families, they have found an emotionally charged way to lead the public to support legislative and ballot initiatives that oppose the enhancement and enforcement of civil rights protections.

Result: Along with immigrants and welfare recipients, lesbians and gay men are scapegoated as the cause of social and economic problems. A primary purpose of the attack against lesbians and gay men is to get the public to think of all civil rights as "special rights" that "majority" people have the power to withhold or bestow on deserving or undeserving "minorities." The Right has altered the definition of civil rights to mean protections one is given based on deserving behavior that will then, supposedly, give a person immediate preference and gain in the job market—and linked these rights to deserving or undeserving behavior of minorities which must be approved by public vote. In so doing, the Right has thrown fundamental civil rights on the public auction block. Rather than remaining the cornerstone of democracy, these rights now are turned over to media-driven, fear-based campaigns that are won by those with the most money and ability to sway public opinion. In the end, any group (such as immigrants and welfare recipients) that is stereotyped as engaging in bad behavior—associated with crime, drug use, teenage pregnancy, etc.—can have its rights eliminated by current public sentiment taken to the voting booth.

• **Welfare Reform**. Well before President Clinton vowed to "end welfare as we know it," there was a movement to remove the safety net for the poor by eliminating welfare and requiring them to find work in a job market that has been decimated by corporate globalization. Under the guise of welfare "reform," as conceived by the Right in 1995 and 1996, there are efforts to limit benefits to two years, require fingerprinting of recipients, require identification of the fathers of children, eliminate benefits to teenage mothers, require "workfare," limit the number of eligible children to two per family, and reward employers for employing recipients rather than recipients for their work produced. Rather than efforts to eliminate poverty by raising the standard of living for everyone, the standard now is to punish the poor for being "undeserving" of assistance.

Result: Welfare recipients, usually portrayed as people of color, are being scapegoated as a primary cause of economic and social problems in the U.S. As poor people they also become targeted as a major cause of social problems as the general public is led to think they, more often than non-welfare recipients, engage in criminal activity such as theft, drugs, homicide, alcohol, and welfare fraud. Poor people in general are depicted as being on the take and unwilling to work. The survival of poor people is threatened by the lack of financial support for their basic needs of shelter, food, and health care.

• **Immigrants**. There is growing opposition both to undocumented immigrants and to the numbers of documented immigrants who are also people of color coming in through the western and southern borders of the U.S. They are portrayed as a threat to American jobs, a drain on social services, and a cause of overpopulation and criminal activity. Meanwhile, the corporate farm economy of most states uses low-paid undocumented immigrant labor to keep profits high and to maintain food prices that are among the lowest in the world. In contrast to its sentimentality about the protection of children, the Right is calling for denial of civil rights and public services to U.S.-born children of undocumented immigrants.

Result: As people grow more distressed over economic and social problems, immigrants become scapegoated as the cause of these problems. Scapegoating leads to discrimination and ultimately to violence against its target. Racism keeps the focus on immigrants who are people of color, not on the large numbers of white European immigrants, and this leads to an increased belief that our social and economic problems are racial problems. Because it is impossible to determine who is and is not an immigrant among people of color, then all people of color are gradually considered to be problems. Keeping up the rhetoric of "illegal immigrants" as opposed to "deserving" American-born people of color serves to divide racially marginalized groups against one another. "Illegal immigrants" are posited as people who threaten scarce services and income to other people of color who, because of racial discrimination, experience economic want.

• **Affirmative Action**. Since the Civil Rights Movement of the 1960s, the Right has been feeding racial resentment and economic fears as a way of increasing opposition to affirmative action. In the 1990s, the debate centers primarily around race (with some downplaying of gender) and calls for ending "special privilege," or "special preferences" to "unqualified" applicants for jobs or higher education. Affirmative action programs are talked about inaccurately as civil rights and are accused of practicing "reverse discrimination," leading to the notion of white men as victims and of the pursuit of equality as "unfair." Blaming individual people of color and women for economic dislocation diverts attention from the collective efforts of global capitalists who are responsible for the loss of jobs available to all people.

Framing the discussion of all "race-based preferences" as equally wrong, whether against whites and men or people of color and women, creates the impression that to consider the realities of racism and sexism is prejudicial. It suggests that actions that recognize the existence of racism and sexism create an "unfair preference." The realities of race and gender discrimination are lost and their injustice not addressed. Those who would seek solutions are forbidden even to name the problem since naming, in and of itself, is considered divisive.

Result: Acts of discrimination against those historically excluded from education and the workplace because of their race or gender are allowed to continue without sanction. Eliminating access destroys the gains people have made in moving toward a more just society and destroys hope. The door to democratic participation and economic opportunity is shut more tightly.

• **Public Schools**. Carol Glaser reports in *Sojourner* (Dec 1993, p. 15) on Bob Simonds' promise to the 130,000 members and 1,210 chapters of Cítizens for Excellence in Education, a theocratic Right organization that he heads: "We can take complete control of all local school boards. This would allow us to determine all local policy: select good textbooks, good curriculum programs, superintendents, and principals. Our time has come!" His proof of his movement is the claim that CEE followers won 3,200 school board seats in 1992.

Public schools are attacked from within and without. First, from without. Because of the deliberate destruction of the tax base, more than ever before, schools are fighting for their economic lives among a populace that is suffering from economic distress and is resentful of almost all public expenditures. One strategy has been the attempt to get the public to approve school vouchers, which would provide tax money for families to send their children to private schools and recreate segregation of public schools. In most areas, school budgets have already undergone massive cutbacks, and this final assault on their funding base would no doubt destroy their ability to survive. Another strategy is to support corporate takeover of the schools, to run them like a business by a corporation, or to support charter schools, so that in effect we have private schools paid for by public dollars. (The corporate strategy brings the risk of applying corporate values to the lives of children: Is this child worth the investment of our dollars? Does teaching art and music pay off in the workplace with corporate profits? Does special education add to production potential?) And the third strategy is to sink the schools with expensive lawsuits that deplete their funds through prolonged litigation.

The attack from within is directed toward the curriculum. Theocratic Right school board members and an organized constituency, based primarily in churches, have focused on three primary areas: health and family issues, religion, and nationalism. In each of these areas, not only is there an attempt to censor spoken ideas in the classroom, but a highly successful effort to remove particular books from the curriculum. Thus, for example, a teacher may not be openly gay or lesbian, talk about homosexuality as a sexual identity, or give children books that are written by gay men or lesbians or present their culture. And finally, there are attacks against teachers and their unions which attempt to establish them as the central problem in public education.

Result: Through control of the schools, the Right could limit information through censorship, shape narrow ideas and views of the world, and enforce a rigid and authoritarian hierarchy. With no accountability to the public, they could restrict entrance into the school system to those of their own choosing, rather than making schools available to all children. Religious observance could be enforced. Minority voices and dissent could be easily extinguished. Rather than being granted the right to education, children would have to earn the right through adhering to an authoritarian, anti-democratic ideology. The schools would not be accountable to the general public but only to those who own them.

Because our concept of gaining equality in democratic institutions, the workplace, and public life is built on a foundation of equal access to education, the destruction of public schools would mean that education and the access it brings are limited to only those who can purchase it. If the theocratic Right gains control of schools, then they, in large part, also control the future of the country through the education of the young.

• **Books, Libraries, the Arts**. From the local level to the national, a massive drive for censorship through organized right-wing grassroots efforts demands removal of "offensive" books and materials, files lawsuits, and promotes government defunding of libraries, the National Endowment for the Arts, the National Endowment for the Humanities, and public radio and television. For example, in California Beverly Sheldon (wife of the Rev. Lou Sheldon, director of the influential Traditional Values Coalition) almost single-handedly got the California Department of Education to remove an Alice Walker short story from their statewide assessment test. In the story a rural Mississippi woman who is married to a Muslim is, Ms. Sheldon claimed, "anti-religious and will change students' beliefs and values" and make them question marriage. Without any hearing, school officials removed the story. Entire aspects of the curriculum, such as multi-culturalism, have been labeled by the Right as an affront to our "true American heritage."

The First Amendment is under attack through these and other actions throughout the country as the Right asserts that freedom of speech is leading to the breakdown of traditional family values and patriotism.

Result: Freedom of ideas and expression can be destroyed, particularly the expression of ideas that differ from those held by the people in power. The dissenting or minority voice, essential to democracy, could be extinguished. Without differences and choices, critical thinking cannot survive. Nor can freedom.

• **The Environment**. For the last two decades, leaders of the timber, real estate, and mining industries, as well as ranchers have united to attack and co-opt the environmental movement. More recently, they have provided major funding for anti-environmental groups that comprise the so-called "Wise Use Movement" and for the election of anti-environmental candidates. An example of their goals is their desire to create a national mining system that would allow mineral and energy production on all public lands, including designated wilderness areas and national parks. They also advocate private ownership of national parks. The equation is shifted from one of collective ownership with private uses allowed to one of private ownership with collective use available for a price.

Result: Environmental laws are gradually weakened or eliminated, corporations have fewer regulations on environmentally damaging actions and there is less funding for their oversight, and more publicly owned lands are turned over to private individual or corporate ownership. The environment is left vulnerable to greater exploitation and destruction. Privatization reduces the avenues people have for redress for the damage done to them by practices that endanger community health. Three out of five African Americans and Latinos live in communities that have illegal or abandoned toxic dump sites, according to a study by the United Church of Christ Commission for Racial Justice. Native American reservations are targeted by major corporations seeking new sites for dumping toxic wastes. Public lands such as national parks are being opened up for commercial use. In the name of economic growth, the environment becomes a landscape of disease and death for all of us.

• **Reproductive Rights**. For more than 20 years the theocratic Right has been vigorously opposing women's right to control our bodies. It remains a core issue in their electoral strategies, a litmus test for every candidate they support. They vehemently oppose the *Roe v. Wade* decision (which was based on the right to privacy) and have worked relentlessly to dismantle it piece by piece. They have focused the debate on abortion as murder; the issue of forced sterilization, relevant to so many low-income women, has been overshadowed, as has the issue of personal choice and autonomy free from the state's interference. They have fought women's reproductive rights through legislation, terrorization of clinic workers, doctors and clients, through major ad campaigns, boycotts, the courts, and murder.

Result: Abortion becomes an option only for those wealthy enough to purchase it or for those who are forced to subject themselves to frequently unsafe alternative measures. Reproductive rights, along with sexual autonomy, are a core issue. If one does not have ownership of one's own body—which is all one brings into the world and all that one takes out—then how can any of the other freedoms have full meaning? The right to control decisions concerning one's own body is essential because it forms one of the foundations of autonomy and freedom. Control over our bodies (freedom to make sexual and reproductive choices, to develop and sustain our health, to make decisions about our dying) is directly connected to our self-determination in a democratic society.

• **Sex Education**. The theocratic Right opposes sex education in the schools, and in government-funded programs—anywhere outside the home and religious institutions. In particular, they object to any discussion of homosexuality. Obsessed with sex (like much of the rest of the culture, they focus attention on it at every opportunity), they believe that any discussion of sex and sexuality leads to sexual activity outside marriage and beyond the control of the theocratic hierarchy of God and man.

Result: Information is banned or censored that could help prevent unwanted pregnancies, the spread of HIV and other sexually transmitted diseases, domestic violence, child sexual assault, and that could promote enjoyable sex lives, good parenting and healthy relationships. Not only do they attempt to censor information, as they did with a study of youth suicide by the Department of Human Services because it named gay and lesbian victims, the Right also presents incorrect information, such as that concerning AIDS and condom safety in their abstinence curricula. As with reproductive rights, promoting sex education supports personal autonomy and freedom—and, consequently, the Right opposes it.

• **Multi-culturalism**. In both higher education and public schools, the Right has vigorously opposed teaching multi-culturalism (literature and history of our diverse cultures), arguing that it destroys traditional western values, and has used the inclusion of books about lesbians and gay men in curricula as the emotional organizing point to bring together both white people and people of color to oppose it. Multiculturalism is the belief that people of many cultures live together in this country and their different cultures should be respected and taught as having equal value to the dominant culture. Because multi-culturalism presents all cultures as equally valuable, a student is provided many beliefs and customs to choose from. To find one's way within these choices requires critical thinking—which is essential both to the workings of democracy and to freedom itself. Critical thinking is the major weapon against authoritarianism and fascism. This is the core issue that most frightens the theocratic Right because it is here that control of mono-culturalism, racist nationalism and white male supremacy can be lost. Multiculturalism is a stake driven into the heart of racism.

Result: We could entrench ourselves as a mono-cultural, English-only, white-dominated society in which all those who are different from this "norm" must adapt themselves to white, heterosexual, Christian, middle-class behavior and standards.

• **Violent Crime**. The Right supports greater enforcement of the death penalty and its expansion to cover more crimes. A recent bill before Congress named 54 crimes that would require the death penalty. They support larger police forces, increased jail capacity, mandatory sentences, tougher border patrols, reduction of the age at which juveniles can be tried as adults, fewer legal rights for those charged with or convicted of a crime—while opposing gun control, rehabilitation programs for the incarcerated, and orders of protection for battered women. They consistently link, either overtly or covertly, violent crimes with people of color, despite evidence showing that violent crimes cut across race and class. Omitted from this get-tough-on-crime, pro-traditional-family movement is significant discussion of violence against women who are raped, battered, violently assaulted and killed in large numbers every day.

Result: The public's fears about safety, plus pervasive racism, are used to bring about a call for a more authoritarian government whose police state will save us from violent people of color and social deterioration. While all other public services are being cut back, police forces and jails are being expanded rapidly and filled disproportionately with people of color and poor people. More youth are being tried as adults. The war on poor people and people of color can lead eventually to a police state because as problems become extreme, extreme solutions become palatable. In many states, prisoners are being used to form a free labor pool for private business, while in Alabama, chain gangs have been reinstated. The Right is moving the body politic to a belief that democratic principles can be sacrificed for the sake of our personal safety. For example, many people advocate that teenagers in poor, racially-mixed neighborhoods be forbidden to congregate in groups of three or more. Consistently, the Right connects race with crime and uses racism as a weapon in the effort to destroy democracy.

WHO BENEFITS

Several conclusions are apparent from this discussion of who the Right is. The Right is not just one group, but is a linkage of people and groups that share many of the same beliefs. What may not be so obvious is that many of those beliefs also reside in the general population, including those of us who consider ourselves progressive. The Right is not working in a vacuum as it moves the body politic, including the Democratic Party, to the right. It is working with and exploiting the racism, sexism, homophobia, and financial greed that exist in ordinary people.

Much of the current conservative analysis of our ills masks the fact that it was a combination of corporate greed and governmental policies, particularly under Ronald Reagan's administration, that led us to this time of social and economic crisis. When people are ignorant or forgetful of the cause of their problems, they can be moved easily to scapegoat those closer to them as the source of their dissatisfaction and discontent. They welcome anything that relieves their discomfort and pain, even if it is state violence and loss of freedom.

Meanwhile, free market capitalism runs unchecked, with obscene profits going into the hands of the few, while less and less is spent on services and human needs for the many. And right-wing demagogues, particularly the zealots of the theocratic Right, pave the way for theocratic authoritarianism by eliminating personal freedoms, autonomy, access, participation, and critical thinking—by destroying hope of participatory democracy in America.

Some of us fear that this volatile mix of global capitalism, racial nationalism and the rise of reactionary religious fundamentalism could give rise to neo-fascism in this last decade of the twentieth century. Many of us are reluctant to raise the specter of fascism because the anti-fascist battles of this century have left us with such a sense of human loss and fear of its re-emergence. We are also hesitant because the term has been used so loosely as an epithet, thrown at people or government policies that offend but that do not merge with other authoritarian factors to make true fascism. In a time when right-wing talk-show master Rush Limbaugh refers to feminists as "feminazis," one is inclined to be particularly careful about words.

In unsettled times, however, vigilance about freedom is always mandated. While many of us desire to expand democracy in this country, we also have to be prepared to defend it when under attack. A people warned is a people more prepared to defend and protect the freedoms we hold dear.

Few people agree on a definition of fascism, though the word is broadly used not only to describe the rightist revolutionary movements of Germany and Italy in the 1930s but any mass movement toward authoritarianism and a police state throughout the world. Those who study fascism agree that it involves a combination of nationalism, militarism, racism, charismatic leadership, populism, and religiosity or sense of heroic destiny, with an emphasis on law and order, discipline, ultra-patriotism, hierarchical families and institutions. It is born out of chaos and disorder, emerging at the point when people are afraid and angry and are seeking survival through the creation of order at any cost.

Many of these indicators are now evident in the social and political climate of the United States.

Our fears in worsening economic and social times lead us to be vigilant about the elements that could ignite to create a neo-fascism that serves financial, religious, and military interests and can lead to repressive and even genocidal policies. Recognition of the early signs of fascism allows the possibility of offering an alternative vision of how people can act together to seek answers for creating order from economic and social justice, not the injustice of scapegoating and repression. Instead of building a society on the notion that "there is not enough to go around," and "you are taking something from me," we can build on the idea of being generous and inclusive, of being tolerant, good neighbors who enjoy both individual rights and mutual responsibility. In this atmosphere, fascism cannot thrive.

HOMOPHOBIA AND RACISM: STRATEGIES OF DIVISION

For almost thirty years we have witnessed three major changes in U.S. life: the globalization of the economy, leading corporations to decimate the U.S. labor force; a series of liberation movements—Civil Rights, Women, Lesbian and Gay, People with Disabilities—demanding full standing in a democratic society; and the rise of religious fundamentalism seeking the merger of church and state to create a theocracy in the U.S. The attacks on working people and the redistribution of wealth upward have destabilized this society, and now the theocratic Right is using racism and homophobia as a means to organize the population to accept authoritarianism as an answer rather than inclusive democracy with expanded civil and human rights.

Since the early 1970s, the theocratic Right has launched a political attack against lesbians and gay men, people of color, and feminists that has affected every adult and child in this country.

While our racism, sexism, and homophobia have often separated people in these groups from one another, religious conservatives lump us together. They see people of color, feminists, lesbians and gay men as standing in the way of their goal to merge church and state in order to give legislated dominance to white Christian males who are taught that they receive their authority from Biblical scriptures. Indeed, they portray us as being the cause of the breakdown of order in society. According to their logic, those rights and protections that give us voice in a democratic society are the cause of immorality and social chaos and must be thwarted or dismantled. The Civil Rights Movement's demand that power be shared by all is a block to their authoritarian vision.

Attacking the idea that some people are inferior by race and must be dominated, the Civil Rights Movement issued a call to conscience and to reason. It said that true democracy calls for justice, participation, and freedom. For most of us, indoctrinated to believe in a democracy that supported the interests of white males, this was a new and profoundly moving idea. Imagine: a demand for justice, participation, and freedom. The words rang in our ears.

African Americans were not the only ones to hear the call. It was also heard by other people of color: Asians, Latinos, Native Americans. Other movements were birthed. It became clear to women that if racial discrimination prevented participation in democracy, so then must discrimination based on sex. It was a heady, movement-building idea. Lesbians and gay men looked at our lives, and everywhere we looked, we saw an absence of justice, open participation, and freedom to be who we are. Then the 1969 rebellion of working-class lesbians and gay men against police harassment at the Stonewall bar gave us the historic, symbolic moment to move toward liberation.

The Civil Rights Movement not only marked the way for other great liberation movements, but its very successes led to a reaction against it and all who embarked upon the long and arduous path to equal rights. It was not by coincidence that it was in the late 1960s, during the presidential campaign of George Wallace of Alabama, that we began to feel the impact of the organized Right. In 1980 a combination of the New Right and theocratic Right laid claim to the election of Ronald Reagan.

Since the early successes of the Civil Rights Movement, which gained some racial integration but not necessarily its goal of equality, there has been a constant backlash against it from the Right. The central organizing focus of this backlash has been to promote the myth that anything gained by people of color in this country must inevitably take something away from white people—that there simply cannot be enough jobs or education or even rights to go around. It is the myth of scarcity played on a racial theme, orchestrated in the context of loss of income and jobs due to economic changes.

In the 1970s, a focus of the backlash was affirmative action, the program that was designed to provide remedies for past discrimination, offering the possibility of equal opportunity. Affirmative action was portrayed and interpreted by many in the white community as an unjust program affecting mostly people of color that took jobs away from talented and skilled white men and gave them to "unqualified" people of color and white women. By 1990, when David Duke talked about "special rights" in his Louisiana gubernatorial campaign, everyone knew he was talking about the so-called "threat" to the white race posed by people of color.

It took only a short step in 1991-92 to build on this perceived sense of white loss by using the "gay rights are special rights" argument to suggest that lesbians and gay men are just one more undeserving minority group trying to take away "deserving" white men's (and in this case, all heterosexuals') rights.

Though there are undoubtedly many people who have moral reservations about homosexuality based on religious teachings or based on ignorance about sexuality in general (and even more about homosexuality in particular), I believe that people are being deliberately manipulated and their homophobia heightened to meet the Right's ends. Homophobia meets the Right's needs in several opportunistic ways:

• The Right has found a golden goose for fundraising by using misinformation and direct lies about the supposed sin, sickness, disease and militancy of lesbians and gay men to create fears and hysteria.

• The Right, building upon the homophobia that people in communities of color share along with white people, can recruit some people of color to act against members of their own community, to act against lesbians and gay men in general, and to make allies with those who have traditionally oppressed them, thereby becoming participants in their own oppression.

• The Right, enhancing a sense of scarcity in people of color who have experienced unrelenting oppression and exploitation, can recruit some people of color to act as the moral gatekeepers of civil rights, declaring who does or does not "deserve" them.

• The Right, relying on the white population's recognition of coded racial language ("no minority status" and "no special rights") in anti-gay and lesbian ballot initiatives, can bring racial hatred into the fight against homosexuality and move both its racist and homophobic agenda simultaneously, thereby opening up the territory for eliminating civil rights protections.

THE ATTACK AGAINST LESBIANS AND GAY MEN, BISEXUALS, AND TRANSGENDER PEOPLE

Introducing homophobia into the mix of racist and sexist backlash has been effective. Focusing on this nation's ambivalence about sex and sexual freedom, the theocratic Right has had great success in coalescing people and developing a constituency when they concentrate on abortion and homosexuality. Both are highly charged emotional issues. Because there is so much confusion and lack of understanding about both abortion and homosexuality, the Right can manipulate information and emotions to gain support for its sexist agenda. The lesbian and gay community makes a vulnerable target because as a people we have had visibility only since Stonewall in 1969. A little more than two decades is a very short time for the general public to gain knowledge of a group. Consequently, false and distorted information can be fed to people who are generally unaware of anything but the most vulgar stereotypes about us.

Many of the strategies for destroying civil rights efforts for lesbians and gay men could be summarized by the title of the popular film, "Sex, Lies, and Videotape." A stunning example in the Right's well-funded and widely distributed videos is the use of mis/disinformation to divide people against one another and to bring bigotry to the ballot box. An analysis of these videos reveals themes common to the Right's overall work to destroy the rights of women, people of color, and lesbians and gay men.

The Right's "Gay Rights/Special Rights" video introduces the race connection and furthers the demonization of lesbians and gay men. This Traditional Values Coalition video begins with footage of Dr. Martin Luther King, Jr.'s "I Have a Dream" speech and goes on to position gay men and lesbians as the enemies of people of color. The video depicts those seeking liberation for gay men, lesbians, bisexuals, and transgender people as those who will "further beat down minorities" and "undermine and belittle" the Civil Rights Act. They position themselves—the Citizens United for the Preservation of Civil Rights—as the long-standing allies of communities of color (although the civil rights voting record of their key spokespeople contradicts this assertion). There are repeated messages that extension of civil rights protections to gay men and lesbians will destroy the civil rights gains of people of color.

In the Right's usual fashion of misrepresentation of the facts, it compares the alleged affluence and privilege of gay men and lesbians to the economic devastation that is the reality of all too many communities of color. It subtly lays responsibility for this situation at the doorstep of the gay and lesbian community by stating outright that the efforts of gay men and lesbians to ensure their rights make a mockery of the legitimate concerns of communities of color. Further, the video asserts that gay men and lesbians already have equal rights under the First and Fourteenth Amendments and argues that we are not seeking civil rights but "special rights." Gay men and lesbians are portrayed as white, affluent, elitist sexual deviants and the enemies of small business, the community, children and the family. The video repeatedly portrays lesbians and gay men seeking "elevation to full minority status" (and the resulting "special rights and benefits and advantages" that people of color allegedly possess) at the expense of and on the backs of those who fought for civil rights in the 1960s—those to whom the video refers as "true" minorities.

During the first few minutes of the film, all of the spokespeople are African American, frequently filmed standing before the U.S. Capitol; they are followed by white authorities such as Mississippi Senator Trent Lott and conservative leaders William Bennett and Edwin Meese.

After the comments on race and civil rights, the video addresses the immorality and disease of homosexuality, showing footage from the 1993 March on Washington for Lesbian, Gay, Bisexual and Transgender Equal Rights and Liberation. It uses interviews with participants as well as with "authorities" such as the discredited pseudo-psychologist Paul Cameron, combined with images of drag queens, military lesbians and gay men, parents carrying children, people wearing leather and carrying whips, to convey the idea that the March was the site of the new Sodom and Gomorrah.

• **Coded Language**. What does the theocratic Right hope to achieve with this video which it has distributed to thousands of churches, schools, and community organizations, as well as to every member of Congress? It demonizes sexual diversity and creates a wedge in the lesbian and gay population between those who want to be accepted as "just like everyone else" and those who are different and marginalized. It also places a wedge between the gay and lesbian community and people of color, creating a barrier to their support of each other's liberation efforts and their ability to unite in opposition of the rise of the Right.

It serves both of these purposes by advancing the development of coded language for rapid communication of bigoted information that will lead people to join ranks with the theocratic Right in their efforts to legislate discrimination against and exclusion of both lesbians and gay men and people of color.

Coded language stands in for overtly racist or homophobic messages. Most people know the racist coded language in the Willie Horton ad created by supporters of the George Bush campaign. In this television ad, the viewing audience was exposed time and again to the message that Michael Dukakis had paroled an African American rapist and murderer who then raped and killed again. The successful goal was to create a kind of mental shorthand that said rapists and murderers are African American, and liberals are soft on rapists and murderers. In his campaign for governor, David Duke took this theme even further in developing these codes: Affirmative action is coded to mean the loss of "qualified" white people's jobs to women and people of color; drugs and crime are linked with community breakdown caused by people of color; welfare is presented as the cause of the economic crisis brought about by people of color who abuse the system; destruction of the family is associated with feminists who support reproductive rights and lesbians and gay men who, they suggest inaccurately, do not create families.

The Right's anti-gay and lesbian videos have encoded several messages: Pedophiles=lesbians and gay men. Gay rights=affirmative action=special rights=civil rights. People with AIDS=disease carrying perverts. The most emotionally charged of these issues is the sexual abuse of children.

The videos lead viewers to associate all lesbians and gay men with the sexual molestation of children. It is the perpetuation of the "Big Lie" strategy—the lie told so often that it becomes the truth to uninformed people. What is omitted is the well-documented information that approximately 95% of those who sexually abuse children are heterosexual men who do it within the intimacy of family relationships and the trust of community with both boys and girls. Because of this distortion of the truth, our children remain vulnerable to abuse because we warn them of only the least likely perpetrators and we do not warn them about "trusted" heterosexual men, most frequently from within their own families.

This "Big Lie" that lesbians and gay men recruit and sexually molest children is the linchpin of the emotional argument at the center of discrimination against us. Using this argument, the video goes on the offensive to move the discussion of the gay and lesbian movement from the context of civil rights to the context of morality. They depict behavior that most people perceive to be wrong, (e.g., the sexual abuse of children) and then extend that behavior to an entire group of people, so that the viewers conclude each member of the group is immoral. Hence, the images of small children in the March on Washington, juxtaposed with naked men and comments about man/boy love, lead the viewers to think that the central focus of lesbians and gay men is the sexual abuse of children. An entire group of people is named as immoral and devalued as human beings. It requires only a short step to remove or withhold rights and protections from this group and to instigate violence against them.

• **Contradictions**. The Right also suggests that civil rights protections and their enforcement should exist only for those whose differentiating characteristics are immutable, such as race or sex or age. They argue that the Civil Rights Act has only a limited application based on a few key criteria—and key among them is "immutability." They say that sexual identity is a matter of choice, not a matter of who one is, and therefore is not "immutable."

First of all, we do not know how people acquire their heterosexual, homosexual, or bisexual identity, but we do know that people have a sexual identity, and currently lesbians, gay men, bisexuals and transgender people experience extreme discrimination and violence because of theirs. Groups of people who experience discrimination and violence (in this case, a group united and targeted because of sexual identity) need enforced rights and protections simply to approach equality of treatment with the dominant group. Still, the theocratic Right asserts the argument that sexual identity is a matter of choice, not an immutable characteristic (though, interestingly, they do not argue that heterosexuals then must also choose their sexual identity and consequent behavior). To keep people from thinking through this argument, they use inflammatory images and misinformation to dehumanize and demonize lesbians and gay men as sexual predators, just as they have characterized African American men since slavery. Lesbians and gay men become "pedophiles;" African American men become "rapists;" African American women become "whores" and "welfare mothers."

Perhaps because its major goal is the establishment of Christianity as the governmental religion of the United States, when the theocratic Right goes into communities of color it does not discuss choice in another area of major civil rights protections—religion. Many of the early white immigrants to the U.S. came in search of religious freedom, and protection of that freedom has been a fairly consistent principle of this country's beliefs and legal system. That freedom means that people may choose their beliefs and forms of worship, whether it be in synagogue or cathedral or storefront church, whether speaking in Latin or speaking in tongues. It is a matter of choice, and religious freedom is covered under both the Bill of Rights and civil rights statutes. We believe in that freedom so strongly that we grant religious groups tax exempt status, even when they use that status to raise money to mount campaigns of hatred and discrimination. While not "immutable," religion is recognized as deserving protection as a civil right.

That is not to say that homosexuality is the same as either race or religion; it is different. Like religion, however, sexual identity is often invisible; and similar to religion, when unpopular, it is attacked. Along with women, people of color, people with disabilities and religious minorities, lesbians and gay men have experienced historic discrimination, and the methods of discrimination have an identifiable kinship with those of other oppressions, as do the results. We see similar tactics used again and again, from oppression to oppression. They all lead to one group of people being able to define another group and have power and control over them and their lives. They all lead to exclusion from equality and full participation in democracy.

THE EFFECT ON THE GAY AND LESBIAN COMMUNITY

While "Gay Rights/Special Rights" influences the heterosexual audience it was created for, it also creates divisions among lesbians and gay men. Pitted against one another, and with our rights assaulted at every turn, oppressed groups often turn against each other in the desperate scramble to keep what little we have. Because it plays directly to the negative messages about ourselves that we have internalized (as has the rest of the population), many lesbians and gay men who seek acceptance by the larger society condemn those depicted in the video and distance themselves from them. People separate themselves off into "good queers/bad queers," with "bad queers" being those who will not "act normal." Difference becomes viewed as a liability and is perceived as a deliberate act, an affront to the dominant group.

Because the video is so assaultive and the potential for our destruction so great, lesbians and gay men may begin feeling that we are the most victimized minority, establishing a false hierarchy. People then discuss homophobia as the worst oppression and AIDS as the ultimate genocide. In doing so, we isolate ourselves from other oppressed groups and fail to connect with each other in response to the attack that is common to all of us. Focusing on ourselves, we fail to recognize that this attack is not the worst thing that has ever happened to a people. Horrible as it is, it is no more terrible than the daily violence that kills thousands of women each year and damages millions more, than the decimation of communities of color by racist violence and police brutality, than the deaths from lack of health care among the poor, than the loss of Native American lands, than the genocide of Jews. All are terrible. All are connected.

Perhaps the worst danger to our liberation is that our fear, anger, and defensiveness lead us to take on the tactics of the enemy. As the Right attacks our dignity and worth, we respond by attacking those within the movement who are different from us. As they invade our right to privacy, we respond by "outing" our own people. As they pit us against each other for the crumbs of rights and entitlements, we fight each other for recognition that our particular issue (AIDS funding, breast cancer research, civil rights legislation, hate crimes laws, domestic partnerships) is the most important. As they attack our leadership, we attack and refuse to support our leaders. As they distort and silence the voices of oppressed people, we shout down and silence those we disagree with. As they block equality and participation for oppressed people, we subordinate the concerns of women, people of color, and people with disabilities in our movement. In the end, we have to ask, who is served by our tactics? Who benefits most?

Our inability to agree on the answers to these questions fractures our vision and strategies, with activists who participate in some way in what we would define as "the movement" often fighting in disunity and horizontal hostility among ourselves. In particular, we have been divided by sexism, racism, and classism, with lines drawn between men and women, between white people and people of color, between those with livable incomes and the poor. Divisions in the lesbian, gay, bisexual and transgender movement make us less able to unite with others in working against the Right and in building a broad progressive movement. Cut off from our histories and pitted against one another, not only are we divided among ourselves but we are divided from our potential allies, often failing even to recognize them.

USING HOMOPHOBIA WITHIN PEOPLE OF COLOR COMMUNITIES

The white leadership of the theocratic Right depends on the concern people of color have for their families, who are under attack both economically and socially, and on their share in the homophobia that is rampant throughout all of U.S. society. They suggest that only white people are homosexuals and homosexuality is threatening to their families and lives. Lesbians and gay men of color are treated as nonexistent or rare aberrations.

Not identifying their own people as lesbian or gay, and not having seen white lesbians and gay men visibly present in the 1960s movement (despite the presence of closeted gays), some African Americans now ask, "Where were you? Why this sudden interest in the Civil Rights Movement? And how dare you say that race and sexual identity are the same when one can be hidden?" The lesbian and gay community is seen as making sweeping generalizations and broad analogies in its desire to get support in the face of current right-wing attacks. Communities of color are saying, in return, "Why should we support someone who just discovered us?" Because of unchallenged homophobia in communities of color and because of persistent white racism, the central issue of civil rights protections for all is lost.

Instead, homosexuality is often perceived in communities of color as a "white thing." This means that lesbians and gay men of color are rendered invisible not only by the white lesbian and gay community but by their own people of color communities as well. It means that when the Right picks up a small economic marketing survey of middle-class lesbians and gay men and then characterizes all of us as being well-to-do, communities of color say, "How can those rich white people compare their oppression with ours? Why should they be concerned about discrimination in employment or public housing when they can buy their way in?" It begins not to matter that the assumption of wealth and race is false. What matters is that these interlopers are "hijacking" the Civil Rights Movement and trying to get something they don't "deserve."

It is indeed true that some white lesbians and gay men are wealthy because white privilege and the ability to hide their homosexuality gave them access to education and job opportunities that racism has withheld from most people of color. Unfortunately, some of the white gay and lesbian leadership helped create this impression by embracing a marketing strategy that depicted themselves as the "normal" white kids next door with dual incomes. However, we have no way of ascertaining the income of the millions of lesbians and gay men who are afraid to identify themselves on questionnaires. Often the most visible people in our communities are those who have the most privilege; therefore the ones we hear from most are white, male, and financially secure, not the lesbians who receive traditional women's wages, the gay men and lesbians of color who receive the wages marked by racism, the poor white gay men, the lesbians or gay parents who fear they will lose custody of their children, and in particular, all of those who find it most difficult to pass as straight.

The error in this entire debate is the failure to recognize that civil rights should be applied justly to everyone, and with heightened awareness toward those who experience discrimination and violence. Hence, we should be acutely aware of how people of color and lesbians and gay men are faring in this democracy because a measurement of a free society is the application of justice to those who are marginalized and harmed by the majority.

USING HOMOPHOBIA AGAINST PEOPLE OF COLOR COMMUNITIES

The Right is known for its stealth tactics and among the most disturbing is their use of racial politics wherein they deliberately omit overt discussion of race in their overall agenda. (In a similar way, they omit discussion of women but attack the programs that support women, such as Aid to Families with Dependent Children, affirmative action, etc.) It has what appears to be a contradictory strategy on race: on the one hand, people of color are scapegoated as the cause of social and economic problems; on the other, it recruits people of color as conservative voters and spokespeople for "traditional family values." The Right uses coded racial language (as well as religion and homophobia) to win the support of the white population and uses religion and homophobia to win the support of communities of color. It works on many fronts to increase the divisions between white people and people of color, to foster conflicts between and among people of color, and to recruit people of color into its ranks. In their vision of social control, race becomes the bedrock that discrimination is built upon, and racist fears are a major motivation for people to join the Right in its movement to reject inclusive, participatory democracy.

Perhaps the most pernicious of these stealth tactics is the reconciliation strategy, whereby groups such as the Christian Coalition, the return-to-male-supremacy Promise Keepers, and even the Southern Baptist Convention make some acknowledgment of past harm done to people of color and then aggressively recruit them into their white ranks. This strategy goes right into the churches, particularly the African American churches, the heart of their community and traditional place of justice-centered organizing. What better way to bring a death blow to any hope for community stability than to compromise the very place that traditionally is the center of hope, unity, stability and, during and since the Civil Rights Movement, has been the place where people rally and organize?

The theocratic Right is particularly active in fundamentalist churches within communities of color, using the same kind of biblical arguments against lesbians and gay men there that were used against African Americans in my own conservative rural church in Georgia in the 1950s. The theocratic Right works to make the church a place of exclusion and condemnation rather than a place of liberation and acceptance. Their appeal is not to people's social conscience but to their instinct for self-protection.

To coalesce people of color in opposition to lesbians and gay men the theocratic Right delivers the message that lesbians and gay men are trying to get some of the same economic pie and moral position that people of color fought so hard to get, and that there is not enough to go around. They suggest that people of color were clean and upstanding and through their goodness earned their rights during the Civil Rights struggle, whereas lesbians and gay men are evil and sick and are merely trying to take advantage of the history of that movement.

Wait a minute. These are the same people who developed their base during the Barry Goldwater campaign in response to the Civil Rights Movement and then strengthened it during the George Wallace campaign. Are we now to think that they were longtime supporters of civil rights for people of color and to this day are out there promoting equality? These are many of the same people who supported, and still support, ex-Klansman David Duke. One of their major spokespeople is Pat Buchanan, who suggested that M-14s would be an adequate solution to the uprising in L.A. following the Rodney King verdict. It cannot be coincidental that these people are now posing as the promoters of racial equality and trying to establish a common enemy through the promotion of homophobia.

It is also through the Black church that the Right seeks its larger victory in combining racism and homophobia to strike a blow against both people of color and lesbians and gay men. It is here where the Black congregation is asked to take a stand against the "immorality" of homosexuality, dividing the church against its own gay and lesbian members about whom it has historically been tolerant and accepting but silent. It is here in this place of solace where African Americans have historically found community that the congregation is asked to view lesbians and gay men (so-called "militant homosexuals") as being financially privileged white people who want to "hijack" the Civil Rights Movement and take away the rights Black people sacrificed so much to gain. It is an outrageous manipulation—a perfect crossing of homophobia and racism.

The Right's tactic of mis/disinformation is used to wedge apart allies and destroy the potential for multi-issue movement building. Homophobia becomes a means to encourage people of color to act against their own best interest. It is mirrored by racism in the white lesbian and gay community.

What the Right does not talk about in communities of color is the Right's opposition to issues that directly affect those communities: to affirmative action for anyone, to workers' rights, to welfare, to government-funded programs that support families, to human rights for immigrants, to equal access to public education, to multi-cultural education, to HIV/AIDS education that would prevent the dramatic increase in deaths of people of color.

The Right uses expedient strategies to organize people around their prejudices. In people of color communities they scapegoat lesbians and gay men as the cause of social and economic problems. In white communities, they scapegoat people of color as the cause of these problems. For example, in California, Asian and Latino immigrants are attacked as a "burden" on health services, school systems, and welfare, causing these systems to break down. While attacking affirmative action as a critical source of economic problems, the Right does not talk about who is really taking the jobs of working-class people: those who make obscene profits by moving their production to countries of color where they pay subsistence wages for the manufacture of goods. Ironically, those goods are then brought back here to sell to people who are daily losing their jobs to a "cheap" labor force in a Third World country. Affirmative action is not closing down plants and businesses in the U.S., unrestrained greed is.

Focusing people's attention on the civil rights effort of lesbians and gay men is a shrewd way of diverting attention from the real social and economic issues of our time and undermining any progress made under the Civil Rights Act. While the theocratic Right talks about morality, I believe they oppose HIV education because they consider the people currently most affected by AIDS as being without great value: gay men, poor women, and people of color. While they talk about protecting the well-being of communities of color, they oppose universal, government-funded health care.

When the Right talks about protecting families, I believe they care about only certain kinds of families, narrowly defined as undemocratic, authoritarian units of social control—those families headed by a male whose power and authority are unshared and unchallenged. Despite the Right's current recruiting drive in communities of color, people of color are not considered part of that "traditional family" the Right so reveres and tries to protect from the encroachment of lesbians and gay men. For example, without mercy or compassion or respect for family units, slavery assaulted African American families by dividing them according to individual workers or "breeders." African American families have survived against terrible oppressive odds, developing new definitions of family and bonded/blended relationships. Many of these families, by their inclusiveness, are not considered proper "traditional families" by the theocratic Right. Instead, the Right stereotypes and condemns them along with Native American, Latino, and Asian families as fostering illegitimacy, crime, and welfare dependency.

Is their concern really about protecting communities of color from lesbians and gay men and about strengthening the family in these communities? If the Right cares about families, why are they not mounting a national campaign against violence against women and children and against alcohol and drug abuse, two of the most destructive issues in family life today in both white and people of color families? If they care about families, why are they ripping apart the families of Mexican and Asian immigrants? Why are they not campaigning for better jobs and benefits for workers? If they care about the effect of crime on our society, why do they support the creation of more jails rather than crime prevention through job training and job development? The solution to our economic and social problems is not the promotion of increased discrimination.

Struggling families are eager for help, but offering false moralizing and false enemies does not help. With a tone of self-righteousness, the Right attributes the "breakdown" of families to immoral behavior, suggesting that "good" Christians in "traditional" families care more for their families than do others. This analysis is insulting to the majority of families in this country. What the Right fails to acknowledge is that millions of people who love their families passionately are separated from them most of the day because the adults and oldest teenage children have to work two or more jobs in order to survive economically. Nothing has hurt families more.

People of color are being positioned as the primary enemies of law and order, economic promise, and community stability. Consider, for instance, how many so-called problem areas are *racialized* in coded language by conservatives and the Right: immigrants, welfare recipients, drug dealers and users, candidates for affirmative action, teenage mothers, criminals, gang members—and poverty itself. Each is a code word for people of color. The general public is led to believe that the majority in each of these categories are people of color, and white people— particularly white women—are erased from consciousness. The racialization of issues is used to mobilize white people, particularly disaffected white men, to embrace the Right's agenda.

It is true that people of color communities have been seriously destabilized since the end of the first wave of the Civil Rights Movement: by white flight from urban to suburban areas, which created a gross reduction in tax money available for urban services, police protection, home building, and the creation of businesses; by the influx into inner cities of drugs that numb the sensibilities of users and also provoke violence; by insurance and bank red-lining; by reduction or elimination of public services to the inner cities; by loss of job and educational opportunities. Any negative economic impact that has hit white communities hard has hit people of color communities several times harder. Rather than being the primary cause of this country's economic and social problems, people of color have been the primary recipients of them.

THE LARGER AGENDA

The lethal combination of racism and homophobia jeopardizes the freedoms we seek. The theocratic Right is expending an enormous amount of time and money in its fight against the extension of civil rights protections to lesbians and gay men. It is now clear to almost everyone that there is a larger agenda than just the repression of a small percentage of our society. Why else so much effort to dehumanize and scapegoat one minority group? What is the larger agenda?

In 1992, when major anti-gay and lesbian ballot initiatives appeared on local and state ballots, we did not fully grasp the larger agenda, but we know far more now than we did then as the markers of social change have rushed by us. We now perceive—we hope not too late—the goal of these efforts by the Right.

Who would have thought that in such a short time civil rights would be redefined in the popular mind and put to the vote at the ballot box? And that the Right would be clever enough to use ambivalent feelings and bigotry against lesbians and gay men as the centerpiece in its attack against civil rights and particularly against people of color?

When the Right put forth its two major anti-gay and lesbian initiatives to amend the constitutions of Oregon and Colorado, some of us realized that they were attacking civil rights and democracy. But I do not think most of us realized how these seemingly outrageous initiatives were plowing fertile ground in preparation for full-fledged attacks against people of color—that, for instance, these initiatives were laying the groundwork for California's anti-immigrant Proposition 187 in 1994 and for that state's recent anti-affirmative action initiative, both to be replicated across the country through legislative and electoral strategies.

Here's how they did it. In the text of their anti-lesbian and gay ballot initiatives and the rhetoric of their videos, the Right concentrated on the ideas of "no special rights" and "no minority status" for lesbians and gay men. Their goal was to muddle the public's thinking about what civil rights really are and to confuse them with affirmative action programs. They played upon this nation's general ignorance about civil rights—that civil rights laws (laws that support the right to be free from invidious discrimination) forbid people (usually employers, landlords, operators of public accommodations, etc.) from discriminating on the basis of specific characteristics. Their vehicle for creating confusion was the manipulation of legitimate anger about loss of jobs in a changing economy into anger at affirmative action as the cause of that loss. This anger was already part of the racist backlash against the Civil Rights Movement, again enhanced by the campaign slogan of Louisiana Klansman, David Duke: "Equal rights for all; special rights for none."

As they laid out the issue, they said lesbians and gay men must be prevented from achieving "minority status" that would make them eligible for *affirmative action* and *quotas*, thus deliberately confusing civil rights with the *program* of affirmative action, and equating civil rights with the "special right" of affirmative action. Though there is no legal category of "minority status" (a term they created for their own uses), the 1964 Civil Rights Act did create remedies and provide enforcement of protections for *all people* who are discriminated against based on their race. Groups historically discriminated against at last had a vehicle to move toward a semblance of fair participation. They introduced the word "minority" in order to keep everyone thinking of race (and gender only secondarily) and the "special rights" people of color supposedly have received.

I remember the confusion of lesbians and gay men in Oregon about the initiative's prohibition of affirmative action. "Why are they talking about affirmative action? We've never sought affirmative action at any time," we said. Little did most people know that they were going for bigger fish than the lesbian and gay community—that they were preparing the ground for the elimination of affirmative action altogether, targeting, in particular, people of color and taking aim at women as well.

But the Right's strategy was even more sophisticated and complex. After creating the confusion about civil rights through a massive propaganda blitz where the words "special rights" were used at every possible opportunity, they also introduced in the initiatives and videos the idea of minorities "deserving" civil rights and attached the prerequisite of *good behavior.* They argued that, first of all, lesbians and gay men are not a "true" or "legitimate" minority because homosexuality is not an immutable characteristic; in fact, the Right says, without any supporting evidence, it is a choice of bad behavior. Then, with blatant misinformation and scapegoating, they argue that lesbians and gay men do not *deserve* civil rights because we are "pedophiles and carriers of disease," i.e., we engage in (or personify) bad behavior.

The concept of behavior dictating whether or not one "deserves" civil rights forms the bridge for the re-thinking of civil rights for people of color. Since almost all so-called bad behavior (crime, drugs, illegal border crossings, welfare fraud) has been racialized, we are led to conclude that most "minorities" do not "deserve" civil rights.

And finally, they argue that the issue of who "deserves" civil rights should be put to the popular vote to amend state constitutions and thereby establish discrimination as a legal principle.

Omitted from this argument is the fact that the Constitution does not require that civil rights be deserved or earned; they belong to all in the nation. Whether they are applied and enforced justly is the issue. The most important pieces of the Right's arguments are these: *civil rights are special rights for minorities (who meet specified criteria) which must be earned through good behavior and can be forfeited by bad behavior.* Now add to this formula right-wing thinking such as is expressed in *The End of Racism: Principles for a Multi-racial Society* (1995) by Dinesh D'Souza of the American Enterprise Institute (a right-wing think tank) which names the primary problem of African Americans as "civilizational" breakdown, i.e., their "uncivilized" behavior. Add also *The Bell Curve* by Charles Murray and Richard Herrnstein (1994) which re-introduces the idea of eugenics (improving hereditary factors through controlled mating), and we have the theory that supports the practice of limiting civil rights and human services and of creating totalitarian control. *The Bell Curve* argues that people of color are destined for poverty and crime because of their low mental capacity which is biologically based and immutable. Further, combining corporate values with the eugenics argument, they suggest that resources should be allocated based on ability to produce (or create a "profit").

With this argument, backed by general lack of information and compounded by the confusions created by the ballot initiatives and videos, the ground is prepared for elimination of civil rights and programs to level the playing field for poor people, such as Head Start and minority scholarships, Aid to Families with Dependent Children, services for the poor, HIV/AIDS prevention programs, affirmative action, services and protections for immigrants. At the same time the climate is set for establishing larger police forces, more prisons and stiffer penalties for crime. The so-called bad behavior of people, especially poor people and people of color, renders them undeserving of fairness or justice. Anything that controls them becomes acceptable or perhaps even a social imperative.

In the current debate about the civil rights of lesbians and gay men, it is important to understand that it is legal for the government or private citizens to discriminate *unless* there is a specific law prohibiting such discrimination. Therefore, in states and cities where there are not laws prohibiting discrimination against gay men and lesbians, it is perfectly legal to discriminate. The Right has set out to make it impossible for gay men and lesbians *ever* to have laws prohibiting discrimination against them.

If it can be established that any one group of people in this country does not "deserve" civil rights and therefore can be legally discriminated against, it calls into question whether other groups "deserve" civil rights. If civil rights can be seen as something one group of people can grant or deny to another group, then it follows that these rights can be brought to a popular vote for any other group. The current trend toward constitutional amendments through ballot initiatives suggests that by the end of this decade, many civil rights laws could be put to popular vote for reconsideration. If civil rights can be defined as "special rights" and the original U.S. Constitution held up as a sufficient, all-inclusive document (exclusive of the Bill of Rights), then not only civil rights for people historically discriminated against, but the Bill of Rights itself, will be in the line of attack.

In a few short years, the Right, through fostering and manipulating homophobia, has introduced ideas that have moved the voting public to support the destruction of civil rights, equality programs, simple justice, and human services—to the peril of not just people of color and the poor but everyone who wishes to live in a free and just society.

OVERCOMING DIVISIONS, BECOMING ALLIES

Community by community, the theocratic Right works skillfully to divide us along fissures that already exist. It is as though they have a political seismograph to locate the racism and sexism in the lesbian and gay community, the sexism and homophobia in communities of color. While the Right is united by their racism, sexism and homophobia in their goal to dominate all of us, we are divided by our own racism, sexism and homophobia—and divided, we are falling.

Many people in the United States are horrified by the current targeting of people of color, lesbians and gay men, women, and the poor as scapegoats for our social and economic problems. It has led some to make comparisons to the early days of Nazi Germany and sound the alarm about the path to genocide that scapegoating can travel. It is not unusual to hear people hold serious discussions about the possibility of moving to another country before it is too late. One can debate whether these reactions are exaggerated or appropriate, but there is little room for debate about the scapegoating taking place and the political and moral concerns it brings with it. Our fears are heightened because we know scapegoating is central to the development of fascism.

One could also argue that lesbians and gay men are at the heart of scapegoating, since the attacks against us are so overtly bigoted and discriminatory, the arguments so hate-filled and irrational. Whether we are central or not, we are the express lane to accomplishing the anti-democratic agenda. For scapegoating to be effective, those near the center of the attack must have a reduced capacity to respond or to defend themselves, either because their numbers and resources are too few, because they are destabilized and divided against themselves, or because they are struggling to meet survival needs and cannot always attend to the larger political assault. Hence, heterosexual people of color, lesbians and gay men of all races, and low-income women are linked together as targets of scapegoating as well as pitted against each other in the struggle for "moral" ground.

Though many in the U.S. are now scapegoated in the attacks from right-wing elected officials and organizational leaders, I believe that people of color are closest to ground zero as the targets of those who would replace democracy with theocracy. Those who would merge church and state to achieve fundamentalist authoritarianism, in pursuit of power and financial control for the elite, use concerns about the "inferiority" and "immorality" of people of color to forward their agenda. The Right is using its strategy to coalesce white people around their racist fears and economic losses to build a revolutionary movement that radically changes the very tenets of democracy.

We can no longer afford single-issue politics that look at the small picture and miss the big one. We cannot allow ourselves to be diverted from what is the larger agenda of domination. Our only hope for defending the democracy and freedoms we now possess, and creating the inclusive world we want to live in, is to join together in our efforts. This will require recognizing how oppressions and oppressed people are linked—and then how this linkage necessitates mutual solutions.

First, we need internal dialogue in our organizations, in study groups, teach-ins, or conferences. We cannot understand the issues of other constituency groups until we understand them internally. That means, for example, that the lesbian, gay, bisexual and transgender movement must have serious discussions about race and gender, and people of color groups must talk about the role of women and lesbians and gay men within their own organizations and communities. And it means that people of color must address homophobia within their own fundamentalist churches, and white progressives have to deal with the homophobia and racism in the white churches that are the major organizing base for the theocratic Right.

Once we understand the linkage of these issues and take action on them internally, then understanding the basis for making coalition with other groups becomes clearer, and our divisions are narrowed. Coalition work is hard because we are taunted and baited and set against one another by the Right, which keeps drilling the message that exclusion is necessary, that there is not enough to go around, that one person's gain is another person's loss.

There is plenty to go around; the problem is that the method of sharing has not been equalized. We have to understand that if any one group can be left out, then reasons can be found to leave any other group out.

RACISM IN THE LESBIAN AND GAY COMMUNITY

One might expect people of color, both gay and straight, and white lesbians and gay men to be natural allies in the fight against our common oppression and domination. I believe this alliance has been prevented not only by the issues previously discussed but also by the racism in the white lesbian and gay community and the Right's ability to play upon existing race and class divisions.

Part of our work is to acknowledge two fundamental truths: that the white lesbian, gay, bisexual and transgender community shares the racist legacy of this country along with everyone else, and that, for the past two decades, the lesbian and gay community has characterized itself as white and, indeed, mostly male, despite outstanding work on the part of people of color and lesbians. Its marketing of itself has been racist and profoundly class-biased.

If lesbians and gay men of color had their share of leadership and support, communities of color would now recognize the lesbians and gay men among them, and there would be bridges built between the issues of racism and homophobia. Because the white dominated lesbian and gay community has given limited leadership and visibility to lesbians and gay men of color, rarely worked institutionally against sexism and racism, or seldom supported lesbians and gay men of color in their work in their own people of color communities, there is a racist legacy that is now heightened in the glare of the current attack. Consequently, in 1993 when white gay male spokespeople asked for support for lifting the ban on homosexuals in the military and compared the lesbian and gay movement to the Civil Rights Movement, African Americans, in particular, were often resentful.

It seems to me that the most critical group, both as a target and as a hope for being the center of coalition work, is lesbians and gay men of color. Not only are they being targeted by the Right because of their race and sexual identity, but from the white gay and lesbian community they face racism, in the people of color communities they face homophobia, and in both communities lesbians of color face sexism. It is lesbians and gay men of color who know what the rest of us are in dire need of learning: that people of color and lesbians and gay men have far more in common with each other than we do with any single member of the Right. It is people of color—especially lesbians of color—who, because of their experience of multiple oppressions, are positioned to lead us in understanding the linkages of oppressions and the mutual solutions that include all of the parts of ourselves. Lesbians and gay men of color have the capacity to destroy this critical strategy that lies at the heart of right-wing organizing for domination. As in the title of Kitchen Table Press' influential, ground-breaking book, *This Bridge Called My Back* (Cherrie Moraga and Gloria Anzaldua, editors, New York, 1991), lesbians of color are indeed the bridge that can bring us together. However, to do this work they must be provided opportunities for major leadership and resources in both communities of color and white gay and lesbian communities. They cannot be tokenized and asked to be a small piece of integration rather than the leaders of the revolutionary multi-issue, multi-racial, multi-cultural vision they have pioneered in creating over the past two decades.

POLITICS OF INCLUSION

With the leadership of progressive lesbians and gay men of color we can learn to do true coalition and alliance work, the long-term work of relationships. We can recognize the big picture and our connectedness, making it possible to build a progressive movement in this country that includes everyone, where power and resources are redistributed, and everyone gets a fair share. Certainly, everyone has the right and obligation to use discernment in determining social and moral values, but it is general discrimination against any group as a whole that we must work against. Full inclusion and acceptance of differences, without stereotyping and dehumanizing, are issues of morality because they lead to justice evenly distributed. When justice is evenly shared, everyone wins because the world becomes a better place—where everyone is secure in the knowledge that basic rights need not be earned or "deserved," but are generally applied as the safety net for everyone.

Developing the politics of inclusion will not be easy because we have many barriers to overcome and because we have no model for it. But I am convinced that this is the only road to both survival and liberation.

The theocratic Right, on the other hand, has an easier time in creating its politics of exclusion. Recognizing that most people are disturbed by the social and political chaos in the U.S., they offer a harmonious vision of a past which never truly existed. They ask us to look in the rearview mirror to that brief time in the 1940s and 1950s when white soldiers returned from the war, went to school on the G.I. bill, found jobs plentiful and housing available and affordable, and when there was a sense of stability and order. What they call for, of course, is a racist, sexist, and homophobic vision, for this was a time of legalized segregation and racist violence, when male authority was unchallenged by women, when abortion was illegal, and when lesbians and gay men were invisible. They romanticize this time as one of "traditional family values." For many of us, it was the time of family horrors when rape, battering, incest and alcoholism were kept as secrets within the family. It was at this time that we began to see nuclear families and their supportive extended families begin to unravel because of the corporate demand for mobility. Nevertheless, the theocratic Right unites frightened and uninformed people in a nostalgia for a past when social order and benefits for the few were bought at the expense of many.

Our vision of inclusion is built on the future, not the past; we are creating that which has not been before. If we can understand that the Right uses divisiveness to destroy our vision of inclusion, then we can learn that our most effective work of resistance and liberation is to make connections, both politically and personally. Making true connections may be the most cutting-edge work for the 1990s and beyond.

While many progressive people agree that we must work against racism, classism, sexism, homophobia, and anti-Semitism, I'm not sure that we always understand how intricately these oppressions are linked and how deeply they are connected to our very survival. For instance, do white lesbians and gay men truly understand that fighting against racism is key to our freedom? As we pursue liberation, we will have to build politics of connection from those glimpses we get of our shared destiny with other oppressed people. As do most people, I came to this recognition from personal experience which showed me both the connections and a vision for what could be.

When I was a senior in high school in 1957 in Lawrenceville, Georgia, I was wildly in love with playing basketball and wildly in love with a girl—and trying to figure out what was wrong with me. In my small farming community of white Christians who believed in a literal interpretation of the Bible, there was no context for figuring out who I was as a lesbian or how to live a whole and complete life.

In my confusion and isolation as a young lesbian, I joined my girlfriend in double dates with our steady boyfriends at the end of their football games. Afterwards, we two girls went home together in sanctioned "spend the nights" where we expressed the love and sexual feelings that were most true to our developing sexual identities. We were deeply conflicted and secretive. We all watched the film, "Rebel Without a Cause," and then, mirroring the film, night after night took our older brothers' cars out on lonely roads to play "chicken." As we barreled down abandoned roads at 80 to 90 miles per hour head-on toward our friends in another car, daring the other to be the first to avoid the impending collision, you can bet I was identifying with James Dean, not Natalie Wood. Confused and distressed, I had deep inside me a sense of abandon and a desire to risk my life because I couldn't make any sense of it. I thought there was something profoundly wrong with me, so much so that I could never expect a place of rest and acceptance among people I loved.

Little did I know in 1957 that 500 miles due west in Little Rock, Arkansas, Mrs. Daisy Bates, head of the NAACP, was organizing a team of African American teenagers to perform an act of courage that would give me my life. Each day, with awesome dignity, Mrs. Bates and the "Little Rock Nine" walked through crowds of jeering, hostile white people and National Guardsmen to demand that quality education be an equal right for all, not an entitlement for white people only.

Though their people had been denied access and equality for centuries, these young people found the courage to stand in the face of hatred to demand that the door of education be opened to everyone. Their actions were one of the bold steps of the early Civil Rights Movement that came to change the lives of all oppressed people, of all people in the U.S. Certainly it changed mine. It gave me my life. The Civil Rights Movement, along with the women's and lesbian and gay movements, gave me the understanding that I am a person of worth and dignity. Because of these great movements that called for justice, participation, and freedom for all of us—including this queer girl from a poor Southern family—I was able to put the pieces of my life together to make a whole.

Sometimes I feel our work is like that of celestial navigation. Before directional instruments were invented, sailors navigated the seas by fixing their compass on the North star; however, if they fixed on the wrong star, then everything thereafter was off course. We are working against years of society fixing on the wrong star. This nation has built all its institutions and policies from the starting point of a fundamental lie: that certain groups of people are inferior to others and hence should be subordinated to them. Every direction taken from this fundamental lie puts us off course, and group after group is lost. If one begins with the lie that people of color are inferior to white people, then it makes equal sense that women are inferior to men. And so it goes. It is our work to fix upon the truth: that all people are of equal worth and deserve justice.

REFLECTIONS ON LIBERATION

Liberation politics: seeking social and economic justice for all people; supporting inclusion, autonomy, choice, wholeness; building and honoring relationships; developing individual and institutional integrity, responsibility and accountability; redefining and sharing power.

These political times call for renewed dialogue about and commitment to the politics of liberation. Because a truly democratic society is always in the process of redefining itself, its evolution is fueled by struggles for liberation on the part of everyone wishing to participate in the development of the institutions and policies that govern our lives. Liberation requires a struggle against discrimination based on race, class, gender, sexual identity, ableism and age—those barriers which keep large portions of the population from having access to economic and social justice, from being able to participate fully in the decisions affecting our lives, from having a full share of both the rights and responsibilities of living in a free society.

The politics of domination idealizes and promotes the values of being separate, of being elite, of being responsible for and to only a small group of people. As the Right practices them, such politics bring about not only separation, but deep social divisions, forced rivalry, and mean-spiritedness. The politics of liberation offer us the values of sharing power, of leading a humane life responsible to and for one's fellow human beings and the earth. The one offers oligarchy for the few; the other democracy for the many.

Perhaps the single greatest difference between progressive people and the Right is our belief in democracy. We are the pro-democracy forces facing an anti-democratic agenda. We must seize the language of democracy and use its principles in our lives and work. We are part of an honored tradition of justice-seeking people and stand proudly on the shoulders of those who have gone before us: such great freedom fighters as Sojourner Truth, Mahatma Ghandi, Nelson Mandela, Lillian Smith,

Martin Luther King, Jr., Joe Hill, Fannie Lou Hamer, Mother Jones, Emma Goldman, John Brown. The list goes on and on.

Because the voices dominating this country's leadership speak only of the false "democracy" of the marketplace, rather than the democracy of diverse people living in community, we have to find ways to raise new voices that speak to the transformational and educational political work of building a wider, more inclusive community. Henry A. Giroux, in his compelling article, "Educational Leadership and the Crisis of Democratic Government," states that

> ...the real challenge of leadership is... educating students to live in a multicultural world, to face the challenge of reconciling difference and community, and to address what it means to have a voice in shaping one's future as part of a broader task of enriching and extending the imperatives of democracy and human rights on both a national and global level. (*Educational Researcher*, May 1992, p. 7)

This is the challenge for all of us. The work of liberation politics is to change hearts and minds, develop empathy with and sympathy for other people, and help each other discover how we are inextricably linked together for our common good and our survival on this planet.

Like power, liberation cannot be given; it must be created. Liberation politics requires

• helping individuals to fulfill their greatest potential by providing truthful information along with the tools and skills for using it, supporting their autonomy and self-government, and connecting them to life in community with others;

• fostering both individual freedom and mutual responsibility for others;

• recognizing that freedom demands people always be able to make their own choices about their lives;

• creating a politic of shared power rather than power-over;

• learning the non-violent skills of compromise and mediation in the sometimes difficult collective lives of family and community—in organizations, the workplace, and governing bodies;

• developing integrity in relationships through understanding that the same communal values—generosity and fairness, responsibility and freedom, forgiveness and atonement—must be maintained not just in personal relationships but in the workplace, social groups, and governing bodies;

• treating everyone as a valued whole person, not as someone to be used or controlled;

• maintaining civility in our relationships and being accountable for our behavior;

• seeing cultural differences as life-enhancing, as expanding possibilities;

• placing a broad definition of human rights at the center of our values: ensuring that every person has food, shelter, clothing, safety, education, health care, and a livable income.

Most of us who seek liberation do not believe that the Right will be overcome by force or by mimicking its tactics. In fact, we must *not* take on its language and strategies. We do believe, however, that we have to organize to defend ourselves from its attacks as well as organize to put our own vision of liberation in place. We must establish a proactive agenda that has justice and equality at its core. We believe that this organizing will be slow work because we need to develop political organizations with constituencies who fully understand the choices facing them and who are committed to progressive social change for *all* of us. Otherwise, people will be swayed by whatever the most charismatic leader of the moment says, whatever the most expensive media ads convey, or whatever fear tactic is used against them. Political education, linked with action, is imperative. Our work is developing people, not just ideas—people who are strong, knowledgeable, and courageous enough to take on the work for economic and social justice.

We are seeking ways to bring people together to work on common causes across differences. If, indeed, all oppressions are connected, then it follows that the targets of this oppression are connected as well as their solution. This interconnection leads us to the idea of collaborative efforts to create democratic values, discourse and institutions.

We believe that we will succeed when we collectively create a vision that in practice offers a way of life so attractive that people will not be able to resist it. As progressive people across this country we are working to create a multi-issue, multi-racial and multi-cultural liberation movement; we are trying to redefine our work and bring more integrity to it; we are engaged in developing a clearer, more compelling vision, building stronger relationships among justice-seeking people, and including more people in the process of creating a democracy that works for all of us.

LIBERATING THE LIFE OF THE SPIRIT

In recent years, the Left in this country has been successful in articulating and debating ideas, but not very strong in touching people's spiritual lives. We often talk about the need to change hearts and minds, as a kind of gesture in the direction of the emotional and spiritual life that exists in people. However, I think that what is needed is not just changing hearts and minds but connecting hearts and minds to each other; overcoming the false divisions between mind and emotions, matter and spirit, the intellectual and the intuitive life.

In the mid-1990s, we are seeing a rapid rise of mean-spiritedness, fed by talk radio and television, the rhetoric of cynical politicians, and the embittered disillusionment of people whose hopes and dreams have been destroyed and whose lives feel threatened. It is a mean-spiritedness that seems to feed upon itself, seeking everywhere someone to blame, someone who is the cause of this pain, this disappointment, this failure to succeed. The airwaves are filled with rancor and anger, cynicism and accusation. Recently, I have been asking people to describe the mood of the country. They respond, "depressed, angry, overwhelmed, feeling isolated and cut off, mistrustful, mean, hurt, fearful." To succeed, our organizing must address these feelings.

As progressive and moderate voices are excluded or silenced or mimic this rage and cynicism, I worry about our better selves diminishing from lack of nurturance and support. I think of our better selves as that place where compassion, sympathy, empathy, tolerance, inclusiveness, and generosity reside. What one might call "soul" is the ability to experience empathy and express sympathy toward others, especially those different from or less fortunate than ourselves. It is our feeling intensely connected to, not separate from, humanity. It is a part of ourselves that has to be nurtured and developed.

If access to our better selves could be visualized as a door, I fear that door is gradually closing. All of our strategies for social change will mean very little if we do not have access to that place inside us where generosity, for example, lives. Much of our work has to be focused on nurturing the life of the spirit, on keeping the door to our better selves as wide open as possible.

Cultural work offers one of our best means of nurturing the individual spirit and our sense of connection to others. It is through the creation of art and culture that the spirit is fed and kept alive and our common humanity is expressed and exposed. Through art and culture we enter the lives and experiences of others, gaining the possibility of understanding, the foundation for empathy and sympathy. In a democracy one of the highest goals should be multi-culturalism—the presentation of the experiences and expressions of the many, bringing us together and opening the way for participation in all aspects of society. Multi-culturalism is present when everyone has a voice, and when we present our lives truthfully in a setting of equality.

During this current movement of the Right toward authoritarianism and theocracy, it is not surprising that conservatives are eliminating funding for the National Endowment for the Arts and the National Endowment for the Humanities. Not only is freedom of expression at issue in this defunding strategy ("our tax dollars won't be spent on things that don't support *our* values") but also at issue is the value of art and cultural expression in this democratic society we are developing. The NEA and NEH are institutions designed to make art and culture more inclusive of everyone; they are owned by the public and attempt to represent its diversity, its many cultures and voices. They are critically needed for building and supporting our humanness in this time of dehumanization. Without these national sources of funding, we reserve most of art and culture for the moneyed elite.

In much of our social change work, we incorporate art and culture only as "add-ons"—the concert after a conference, the song or poem at the beginning of the meeting. We rarely see cultural organizing as social change work. One reason is that we are stuck in the same old methods of organizing and do not question how people learn, what moves us to change. Another reason is that we become too focused on a single goal or issue and do not consider the wholeness of ourselves and our constituency. For instance, in building a movement, eating and singing together may be as important as handing out leaflets. Being able to involve our families with us in our work may be as important as recruiting new members. The basis for successful organizing work is people who are connected, not separated, people who feel whole, not fragmented. To insist upon our wholeness is to insist upon our humanity.

In a recent cultural workshop, I witnessed another way of delivering a message about our humanity. A group of my peers struggled with the issue of how, in this time of anti-immigrant sentiment, to help people understand that they were a part of multi-racial, multi-cultural America. The result was a decision to transform several of the most powerful American symbols: the flag, the pledge of allegiance, and the Star Spangled Banner. In a day's time they created a very complex design of a large traditional U.S. flag that had movable parts. It formed the backdrop for their presentation. This multi-racial group of cultural workers marched in the room to the beat of Japanese and Native American drums. They read a re-worded pledge of allegiance and sang a national anthem that were both inclusive and welcoming, offering opportunity and justice. Then they walked up to the flag, and in the rhythmic movements of dance, took it apart, piece by piece, and reconstructed a new flag from the pieces. It became a sun of blended colors with multi-colored beams and sun spots radiating from it. This symbol, with its new design and many colors, now included and represented all of us. It touched places in us that we did not know were accessible. Almost every one of the 30 of us in the workshop burst into tears because of the power of this new image of this country where we had sought recognition and support for our human dignity. We had not fully realized what great power these symbols held for us, or the depth of our feeling for a country that had marginalized so many of us.

Storytelling is one of the strongest traditional cultural expressions that helps us feel whole and connected. Nothing is more critical than storytelling to defining our humanity. Those who control storytelling have power over that definition and our understanding of ourselves. It is essential that we not give over the control of our stories to corporate and right-wing media. When telling our stories, we assert both our individuality and our connection to others, and we make others aware of our identity and history. What better way to counter gross stereotyping, demonizing, and dehumanization than by presenting a multiplicity of voices and experiences, each individualized, each unique, and each connected to a common history.

There are many examples of storytelling—through traditional storytelling, music, art, dance, film, and books—as part of social change work.

Civil rights singer and cultural worker Jane Sapp spends much of her time working with African American children. Sitting at her piano with children grouped around her, she encourages them to talk about their lives, the hard parts, the shining moments, their indignation over injustice, their hopes and dreams. Then she works with them to create songs out of their own histories and experiences. In a matter of a few hours, one can see change in these children's faces, hear pride and enthusiasm in their voices, sense a transformation of spirit. They are building themselves.

In the early days of the women's anti-violence movement, women met in groups to tell the story of the violence that had occurred in their lives. For many, it was the first time they had told anyone what happened—the rape, incest, battering, torture—and telling the story to others brought them out of isolation and gave them connection to a group. But what followed next was the foundation for a women's anti-violence movement: after women heard each other's stories, they came to recognize the great similarities among them. Through discussing these commonalities, they created an analysis of the relationship between the perpetrator of violence and its target, and they recognized that though the victim is frequently blamed for the violence, the fault lay with the perpetrator and the society that accepted the violence. Those desiring to end violence against themselves and other women then moved to take action: creating safe homes and battered women's shelters, hotlines and support groups, working with police, changing laws, confronting batterers and rapists, providing political education and changing public policy. Telling stories is still the very heart of the women's anti-violence movement.

Telling stories provides especially rich results when dissimilar people share stories with each other. This has been our experience with the Women's Watchcare Network at the Women's Project in Little Rock, Arkansas. When we hold meetings in small towns, we bring together people from all of the areas of biased violence that we monitor, and for many it is the first time they have sat in a mixture of Jews, people of color, white women, lesbians and gay men. We have witnessed transformation take place when, for example, an African American gay man tells the story of the violence he has experienced, and an older white churchwoman realizes that it is akin to the violence she has known in her own life. When she recognizes that gay men are hated because they are seen both as being like women and as betraying male dominance, and that their murders are similar in almost every way to the murders of women (overkill, sexual assault, disfigurement), it is an epiphany for her and usually for everyone in the room. By telling their stories, people in these Watchcare meetings become connected through understanding the similarities of the prejudice and violence against them. Once one connection is made, there is an opening for people to begin seeing each other as individualized and fully human.

One of the legitimate criticisms of the Left, or of progressive people, is that we spend too much time talking with each other and not enough time with people who do not share our views. We must find language and access for these conversations; we must take our stories to people who have not heard them, and we must listen carefully and respectfully to theirs. Recently, I had the opportunity, on a plane, to sit next to a rural Oregon pastor who was returning from a large meeting of the Promise Keepers. He said I was the "second homosexual" he had ever met, and he was the first Promise Keeper I had ever encountered. For an hour and a half, we talked about politics and our lives, frankly and with open hearts—sex, dominance of women, pedophilia, economics, violence against women, exclusion of lesbians and gay men from churches, male responsibility, racial injustice. By the end of that conversation, we had inched toward one another in our political/social understanding. Did we agree on core beliefs? No. But in answer to the final question of our conversation—could we live in houses side by side, borrow a cup of sugar over the fence, and let our children play together?—the answer from both of us was yes.

Cultural work keeps us constantly grappling with the issue of values. It is currently popular for politicians and preachers to create a loud din of condemnation on the subject of "traditional values." Much of their focus is on scapegoating particular groups of people as being responsible for the breakdown of these "traditional" values: liberals, feminists, lesbians and gay men. In fact, cultural work and art offer the opposite of scapegoating: the celebration of both the individual and the community, the connections between us all; the possibility of building relationships. When we begin with this foundation (rather than one of authoritarianism and dominance) for determining values, we allow the development of empathy and sympathy which lead us to value generosity, inclusion, kindness, fairness, responsibility for ourselves and others. And these bring us to our great democratic goals of justice, equality, and freedom—for all.

TRANSFORMATIONAL ORGANIZING AND BUILDING COMMUNITY

For whatever reasons, progressive people have not always talked a great deal about the strong moral convictions underlying why we do this work of social justice: *it is because we believe every person counts, has human dignity, and deserves respect, equality and justice.* This morality is the basis for our vision, and when we do our best vision-based organizing (as opposed to response-based or expediency-based), all our work flows from this basic belief.

Ours is a noble history. Because progressive people believe in the inclusion of everyone in the cause of justice and equality, we have struggled for civil rights for people of color, for women, for people with disabilities, and now for lesbians and gay men. We have worked to save the environment, to provide women autönomy and choice concerning our bodies, to end unjust wars, to end homelessness, hunger, and poverty, to create safe workplaces, decent wages and fair labor practices, to honor treaty rights, to eliminate HIV and improve health care, to eliminate biased crime and violence against women and children. We share broad principles of inclusion, fairness, and justice. We must not forget what provides the fire for our work, what connects us in the struggle for freedom and equality.

We are living in a time in which people are crying out for something to believe in, for a moral sense, for purpose, for answers that will bring some calm to the chaos they feel in their lives. As progressive people, we have not always offered up our vision of the world, our activities for justice, as a moral vision. When we have, as during the Civil Rights Movement, people working together for a common good have felt whole.

I believe it is our moral imperative to help each other make connections, to show how everyone is interrelated and belongs in community, or as it is currently expressed, "We all came on different ships but we're in the same boat now." It is at our peril if we do work that increases alienation and robs meaning from life. Today's expressions of violence, hatred, and bigotry are directly related to the level of alienation and disconnection felt by people. For our very survival, we must develop a sense of common humanity.

It may be that our most important political work is figuring out how to make the full human connection, how to engage our hearts as well as our minds, how to heal the injuries we have suffered, how to do organizing that transforms people as well as institutions. With these as goals, we need to re-think our strategies and tactics.

We have to think about our vision of change. Are we involved in a struggle for power that requires forces and resources on each side and a confrontational show-down in which only one side wins? If we are in a shoot-out, then the progressive side has already lost, for certainly there are more resources on the Right at this moment. In other cases where we can organize the most resources, such as the 1992 "No on 9" campaign in Oregon, what is the nature and permanency of the win? The anti-gay and lesbian constitutional amendment was defeated, but in general, people did not have a sense of ecstatic victory. I think there were two primary reasons: 1) the Right immediately announced its intention to take the fight to local rural communities and to build a string of victories in areas where it had developed support—indicating that this is indeed a long struggle for the hearts and souls of Oregonians; and 2) the campaign did not facilitate the building of lasting relationships, of communities, of progressive institutions—because it did not see itself as part of a movement. At the end, I believe people felt a war-like atmosphere had been created, but that the language and tactics of war had failed them. In the months that followed the election victory, people seemed fatigued, wary, often dispirited and in retreat. Rather than being transformed into new politics and relationships by their experience, they seemed battered by it.

• **Transformational Organizing**. There is something to be learned when victory feels like defeat. Somehow, people did not emerge from the Oregon experience with a sense of vitality, of wholeness, of connection. Justice-seeking people must call into question our methods of organizing. Often we have thought that effective organizing is simply being able to move people as a group, sometimes through manipulation, to act in a particular way to achieve a goal. Too often the end has justified the means, and we have failed to follow Ghandi's belief that every step toward liberation must have liberation embedded within it. By concentrating on moving people to action, we have often failed to hear the voice of their spirit, their need for connection and wholeness—not for someday after the goal has been gained, but in the very process of gaining it.

I am not arguing that we should give up direct action, civil disobedience, issue campaigns, political education, confrontation, membership and voter drives, etc. We need to do these things and much more. I am suggesting that we re-think the meaning of social change and learn how to include the long-term work of transforming people as we work for social justice. We must re-define "winning." Our social change has to be more than amassing resources and shifting power from the hands of one group to another; we must seek a true shift in consciousness, one that forges vision, goals, and strategies from belief, not just from expediency, and allows us to become a strong political force.

The definition of transformational politics is fairly simple: it is political work that changes the hearts and minds of people, supports personal and group growth in ways that create healthy, whole people, organizations, and communities, and is based on a vision of a society where people—across lines of race, gender, class and sexuality—are supported by institutions and communities to live their best lives.

Among many possibilities, I want to suggest one way to do transformational work: through building community that is based on our moral vision.

• **Building Community, Making Connections**. Where do we build community? Should it be geographic, consisting of everyone who lives in the same neighborhood? Based on identity, such as one's racial identity, sexual identity? Organizational or work identity? Where are the places that community happens?

It seems to me that community can be created in a vast number of places and ways. What is more important is the *how* of building community. To get to the how, we first have to define what community is. Community is people in any configuration (geographic, identity, etc.) bonded together over time through common interest and concern, through responsibility and accountability to one another, and at its best, through commitment, friendship and love.

To live in authentic community requires a deeper level of caring and interaction than many of us currently exhibit in our drive for individualism and self-fulfillment. That is, it calls for living with communal values. And we face a daunting challenge here because we all live in a culture that glorifies individualism. For example, what the Right calls "traditional family values" actually works against the often-quoted African proverb, "It takes a village to raise a child," which speaks to the communal value of the importance of every child in the life of the community, present and future. Such values point to very different solutions than those currently suggested for the problems of youth alienation, crime, and violence. Rather than increasing police forces and building more jails, with these shared values we would look toward more ways for the community as a whole to be responsible for and accountable to children. We would seek ways to support and nurture their lives. All of us would be teachers, parents and friends for every child.

Creating community requires seeing the whole, not just the parts, and understanding how they interrelate. However, the difficult part is learning how to honor the needs of the individual as well as those of the group, without denying the importance of either. It requires a balance between identity and freedom on the one hand and the collective good and public responsibility on the other. It requires ritual and celebration and collective ways to grieve and show anger; it requires a commitment to resolve conflict.

Most of all, it requires authenticity in relationships between and among whole people. This means that each of us has to be able to bring all of who we are to the relationship, neighbor to neighbor, friend to friend, worker to worker. Bringing all of who we are to community requires working across great differences in culture, in lifestyle, in belief. It demands that we look beyond our own lives to understand the lives of others. It demands that we interact with the lives of others. It requires understanding the connections among people's lives and then seeking comprehensive solutions to multi-issue, multifaceted problems. If we allow only certain parts of people to surface, and if we silence, reject or exclude basic pieces of their essential selves, then we begin designing systems of oppression. Community becomes based on power and non-consensual authority: those who have the most power and privilege dictate the community norms and their enforcement.

One of the goals of every political activity we engage in should be to move beyond superficial interactions to the building of relationships and community. Much of this work is simple, not difficult or complex; it merely requires redefining our values and how we spend our political time. For example, far too often I go to meetings, frequently held in sterile hotel conference rooms, where introductions are limited to people giving their names or, at best, what work they do. Building relationships—whether those of neighbor, friend, lover, work partner—requires that we ask *who are you*? In rural communities in the South and on American Indian reservations, people spend a lot of time talking about who their people are, how they are connected to people and place. Women activists in the housing projects in New Orleans get to know each other by telling their life lines, the major events that shaped them along the way. It is almost ritual for lesbians to get to know each other by telling their coming out stories—when and how they first experienced their lesbianism.

Building connection and relationship requires that we give it time, not just in meetings but in informal opportunities surrounding meetings, structured and unstructured. For instance, when I did political education on oppression issues within the battered women's movement, there was always a dramatic difference in the relationships that were built when we stayed in retreat centers or self-contained places away from distracting outside activities rather than in city hotels. So much of what happened in people's growth and understanding came from living, sleeping, and eating together in an atmosphere that encouraged interaction.

As a way to think about building community, we can ask ourselves these questions:

• In what settings with other people have I felt most whole? What is it that makes me feel known and accepted as who I am?

• What conditions make me most able to work well in partnership with other people? What makes me feel connected rather than alienated?

• What are communal values? What are the practices that support them?

• Where are the places where community is occurring? (For example, in care teams for people living with AIDS, in youth gangs, in certain churches or neighborhoods, in AA groups?) What are the characteristics of these communities?

• Who is being excluded from community? What barriers are there to participation?

• What are the qualities of an inclusive community as opposed to an exclusive community?

• What makes a community democratic?

Our communities are where our moral values are expressed. It is here that we are called upon to share our connection to others, our interdependence, our deepest belief in what it means to be part of the human condition, where people's lives touch one another, for good or for bad. It is here where the rhetoric of belief is forced into the reality of living. It is from this collection of people, holding within it smaller units called families, that we build and live democracy. Or, without care and nurturance, where we detach from one another and destroy our hope for survival.

POLITICAL INTEGRITY AND MULTI-ISSUE POLITICS

It is one thing for us to talk about liberation politics; it is of course another to live them. We lack political integrity when we demand liberation for one cause or one group of people and act out oppression or exploitation toward others. If we do not have an integrated analysis and a commitment to sharing power, it is easy to act out politics that simply reflect a hierarchy of domination.

In our social change organizations in particular we can find ourselves in this dangerous position: where we are demanding, for example, liberation from sexism but within the organization we act out racism, economic injustice, and homophobia. Each is reflected in who is allowed to lead, who makes the highest and lowest salaries, who is allowed to participate in the major decision-making, who decides how the resources are used. If the organization does not have a vision and a strategy that also include the elimination of racism, sexism, economic injustice, and homophobia (as well as oppressions relating to age, physical ability, etc.), then internal conflict is inevitable. People cannot single out just one oppression from their lives to bring to their work for liberation: they bring their whole selves.

Creating a multi-racial, multi-cultural, multi-issue vision of liberation is no easy task. It is much easier to stay within the framework of oppression where our women's organizations' leadership is primarily white, middle-class women, heterosexual or closeted lesbians; our civil rights organizations are male-dominated; our gay/lesbian/bi/transgender organizations are controlled by white gay men and/or white lesbians. And where the agendas for change reflect the values of those who dominate the leadership.

It is easier to talk about "diversity" than about shared power. Or to use a belief in identity politics to justify not including others in a vision for change. I do not believe in either diversity or identity politics as they are currently practiced.

First, diversity politics seem to focus on the necessity for having everyone (across gender, race, class, age, religion, physical ability) present and treated well in any given setting or organization. A core premise is that everyone is oppressed and all oppressions are equal. Since the publication of the report, "Workforce 2000," that predicted the U.S. workforce would be made up of 80% women and people of color by the year 2000, a veritable growth industry of "diversity consultants" has arisen to teach corporations how to "manage" diversity. With integration and productivity as goals, they focus on issues of sensitivity and inclusion—a human relations approach—with acceptance and comfort as high priorities. Popular images of diversity politics show people holding hands around America, singing "We Are the World." People are generally reassured that they do not have to give up anything when they diversify their workplace. They simply have to include other people and become more sensitive to differences.

Because the history of oppression is one of excluding, of silencing, of rendering people invisible, I have great appreciation for the part of diversity work that concentrates on making sure everyone is included. However, our diversity work fails if it does not deal with the power dynamics of difference and go straight to the heart of shifting the balance of power among individuals and within institutions. A danger of diversity politics lies in the possibility that it may become a tool of oppression by creating the illusion of participation when in fact there is no shared power. Having a presence within an organization or institution means very little if one does not have the power of decision-making, an adequate share of the resources, and participation in the development of the workplan or agenda. We as oppressed people must demand much more than acceptance. Tolerance, sympathy and understanding are not enough, though they soften the impact of oppression by making people feel better in the face of it. Our job is not just to soften blows but to make change, fundamental and far-reaching.

Identity politics, on the other hand, rather than trying to include everyone, brings together people who share a single common identity such as sexual orientation, gender, or race. Generally, it focuses on the elimination of a single oppression, the one that is based on the common identity; e.g., homophobia/heterosexism, sexism, racism. However, this can be a limited, hierarchical approach, reducing people of multiple identities to a single identity. Which identity should a lesbian of color choose as a priority—gender, race or sexual identity? And does choosing one necessitate leaving the other two at home? What do we say to bisexual or biracial people? Do we tell them to choose? Our multiple identities allow us to develop a politic that is broad in scope because it is grounded in a wide range of experiences.

There are positive aspects of organizing along identity lines: clarity of single focus in tactics and strategies, self-examination and education apart from the dominant culture, development of solidarity and group bonding. Creating organizations based on identity allows us to have visibility and collective power, to advance concerns that otherwise would never be recognized because of our marginalization within the dominant society.

However, identity politics often suffers from the failure to acknowledge that the same multiplicity of oppressions, a similar imbalance of power, exists within identity groups as within the larger society. People who group together on the basis of their sexual identity still find within these groups sexism and racism that have to be dealt with—or if gathering on the basis of race, there is still sexism and homophobia to be confronted. Whole, not partial, people come to identity groups, carrying several identities. Some of liberation movements' major barriers to building a unified and cohesive strategy, I believe, come from our refusal to work directly on the oppressions—those fundamental issues of power—within our own groups. A successful liberation movement cannot be built on the effort to liberate only a few or only a piece of who we are.

Diversity and identity politics are responses to oppression. In confronting oppressions we must always remember that they mean more than people just not being nice to one another. They are systemic, based in institutions and in general society, where one group of people is allowed to exert power and control over members of another group, denying them fundamental rights. Also, we must remember that oppressions are interconnected, operating in similar ways, and that many people experience more than one oppression.

As I have stated, I believe that all oppressions in this country turn on an economic wheel; they all, in the long run, serve to consolidate and keep wealth in the hands of the few, with the many fighting over crumbs. Oppressions are built, in particular, on the dynamic intersection of race and gender and class. Without work against economic injustice, against the dehumanizing excesses of capitalism, there can be no deep and lasting work on oppression. Why? Because it is always in the best interest of the dominators, the greedy, to maintain and expand oppression—to feed economic and social injustice.

Unless we understand both the interconnections of oppressions and the economic exploitation of oppressed groups, we have little hope of succeeding in a liberation movement. The theocratic Right has been successful in driving wedges between oppressed groups because there is little common understanding of the linkages common to all oppressions. Progressives, including lesbians and gay men, have contributed to these divisions because, generally, we have dealt only with single pieces of the fabric of injustice. Often we have no knowledge of a shared history. We stand ready to be divided. If, for example, an organization has worked only on sexual identity issues and has not worked internally on issues of race and gender, then it is ripe for division on those issues.

As analyzed in an earlier chapter, the Right has had extraordinary success in using homosexuality as a wedge issue, dividing people on the issues clustered around the Right's two central organizing points, traditional family values and economics. It has been successful in using economics to divide "illegal" immigrants from legal immigrants; in using race, gender, and economics to divide people of color and women from low income white men on the issue of affirmative action.

The question, as ever, is what to do? I do not believe that either a diversity or identity politics approach will work unless they are changed to incorporate a multi-issue analysis and strategy that combine the politics of inclusion with shared power. But, one might say, it will spread us too thin if we try to work on everyone's issue, and ours will fall by the wayside. In our external work (doing women's anti-violence work, working against police brutality in people of color communities, seeking government funding for AIDS research), we do not have to work on "everybody's issue"—we can be focused. But how can we achieve true social change unless we look at all within our constituency who are affected by our particular issue? People who have AIDS are of every race, class, age, gender, geographic location, but when research and services are sought, it is women, people of color, poor people, who are most overlooked. The HIV virus rages on because those in power think that the people who contract it are dispensable. Are we to be like them? To understand why police brutality is so much more extreme in people of color communities than in white, we have to understand also why, even within these communities, it is even greater against poor people of color, women who are prostitutes, and gay men and lesbians of color. To leave any group out leaves a hole for everyone's freedoms and rights to fall through. It becomes an issue of "acceptable" and "unacceptable" people, deserving and undeserving of rights, legitimate and illegitimate, deserving of recognition as fully human or dismissable as something less.

Identity politics offers a strong, vital place for bonding, for developing political analysis. With each other we struggle to understand our relationship to a world that says that we are no more than our identity, and simultaneously denies there is oppression based on race or gender or sexual identity. Our challenge is to learn how to use the experiences of our many identities to forge an inclusive social change politic. The question that faces us is how to do multi-issue coalition building from an identity base. The hope for a multi-racial, multi-issue movement rests in large part on the answer to this question.

Our linkages can create a movement, and our divisions can destroy us. Each point of linkage is our strongest defense and also holds the most possibility for long-lasting social change.

If our organizations are not committed internally to the inclusion and shared power of all those who share our issue, how can we with any integrity demand inclusion and shared power in society at large? If women, lesbians and gay men are treated as people undeserving of equality within civil rights organizations, how can those organizations demand equality? If women of color and poor women are marginalized in women's rights organizations, how can those organizations argue that women as a class should be moved into full participation in the mainstream? If lesbian and gay organizations are not feminist and anti-racist in all their practices, what hope is there for the elimination of homophobia and heterosexism in a racist, sexist society? It is an issue of integrity.

In the larger social change community our failure to connect issues prevents us from being able to do strong coalition and alliance work with one another. Most frequently, coalitions and alliances are created to meet crisis issues which threaten all of us. Made up of groups that experience injustice, they should have common ground. They most frequently fall apart, I believe, because of failure in relationships. As in all human relationships, it is difficult to solve the issue of the moment without a history of trust, common struggle, and reciprocity. Homophobia, for example, has kept us "quiet" and invisible in our anti-racist work; racism has kept us "quiet" in our lesbian and gay work. We need to be visible in our work on all fronts. Working shoulder to shoulder on each other's issues enables us to get to know each other's humanity, to understand the broad sweep of issues, to build trust and solidarity.

Our separateness, by identity and by issue, prevents the building of a progressive movement. When we grasp the value and interconnectedness of our liberation issues, then we will at last be able to make true coalition and begin building a common agenda that eliminates oppression and brings forth a vision of diversity that shares both power and resources.

TRYING TO WALK THE TALK: AN EXAMPLE

For the past fifteen years, we at the Women's Project in Arkansas have been trying to figure out how to develop political integrity and to follow a multi-issue agenda. Certainly it has not always been easy, but it has kept us relentlessly growing and learning, has built in each of us a powerful political conviction and determination, and has made all of us feel more whole. And while the organization is not always thought to be correct on all of its issues, it is respected for its efforts to maintain political integrity, internally and externally. We feel that we are participating every day in the creation of democracy and that we are as unfinished as it is, but the dream of justice and equality lifts us up and moves us forward.

The goal of the Women's Project is to eliminate racism and sexism. We believe these two are inextricably intertwined and must be dealt with equally, together, and head-on. We also think that all other oppressions are rooted in economics and connected to these two through similarity of method and intent. As a women's organizing and political education project, we have chosen to focus on economic injustice and violence against women and children as two major areas of discrimination against and control of both women of color and white women. Working on these issues includes working with men and boys and places us near the heart of community work.

In our community and nation our demand is for equality and justice, for shared power and resources, for opportunity and participation, for individual and group responsibility and freedom. In the search for political integrity, the challenge has been to create an internal philosophy and a structure and practice that reflect the vision of the world we seek for everyone.

• **Economics**. Much of our political analysis is focused on economics as the root source of inequality, and we have seen economic injustice at work everywhere. Daily, we witness women unable to leave their batterers because they cannot afford to feed their children. We witness people condemned because of their poverty. We see the poverty of people of color viewed as an indication of their lack of value in society. Hence, we address the internal economic issue first.

We pay everyone at the Women's Project the same salary, no matter what job she does, and no matter how long she has worked there. At any time we have only four to five full-time employees, and pay others such as a bookkeeper, child care providers, and layout designers for the newsletter on an hourly basis at the same rate the full-time staff is paid. Longevity is rewarded with other forms of compensation: a month yearly vacation after two years of employment; a retirement pension after five years; a five-month paid sabbatical after every five years worked.

We believe that an hour of one woman working as hard as she is able is equal to another woman's hard work, no matter what the task at hand, whether it is writing funding proposals, providing care for children, giving speeches, clipping newspaper articles and documenting violence, or cleaning the office. What is most important to us is commitment to the work and working hard. Consequently, we try to be very careful in our hiring. As a community-based, social change organization, our first concern is that a potential employee have a passion for social and economic justice and a desire to give her best self to the job. After that, we look at skills and the way needed skills can be learned during employment at the Project. Using these criteria, we are able to hire women whose life experiences are rich but who may not be formally educated or are inexperienced in a conventional workplace.

Our annual budget is almost $250,000, derived from foundation grants, churches, individual donors and pledges, compensation for services, sales of books and products. Every member of the staff participates in fundraising. This way, we understand where our salaries and resources come from, participate in their creation, and are prepared to make decisions about their distribution.

When describing the organizational structure of the Women's Project, I am often told by people from larger organizations that such a pay structure could work only in a small place. Perhaps so, but a variation on it could also work. Larger organizations could create a policy to allow no more than a 20% differential between the highest paid employees and the lowest paid. If we do not do this, then the structure of our social change organizations reflects the economic pyramid of this country. Those at the apex (the fewest) make the most money and have the most power (control of decision-making and distribution of resources). Accountability should be horizontal rather than vertical. Those at the bottom make the least and are not allowed to take part in the decisions that affect their lives and the life of the organization and its constituency. For instance, it is common in many social change and social service organizations for those who have the most contact with the constituency (battered women, for instance) to make the least money. Those who have the most contact with power (funders, community leaders) make the most money.

• **Historic Inequality: Beyond Affirmative Action**. As a women's organization working to eliminate racism, we try to do what we call "tilting the balance of historic inequality." We live in a country that has systematically withheld access to opportunity and participation from people of color, has practiced genocide, in particular against American Indians and African Americans and blamed them for causing it, has induced poverty, has dealt the blows of substandard education and health care, and has both appropriated the culture of people of color and condemned it as primitive and inferior—all leading to enforced inequality. We do not believe this history of injustice and inequality can be easily overcome, but we try to make major changes both organizationally and individually. We want to change ingrained thinking and assumptions.

We believe that when everything is placed in the balance, racial parity is more than simply creating an accurate reflection of the racial makeup of the population, or balancing 50% white women and 50% women of color. White women belong to only one of many racial groups in this country but that particular group has been the dominant power and has created the historic inequality. Quite simply, once domination has been ingrained for generations, for centuries, it is extremely difficult to throw off its assumptions and behaviors during efforts toward equality. Major structural and policy changes have to be made to ensure and support lasting results. And it is still difficult.

The way we try to tilt the balance is to make the majority of our organization women of color, who earn equal salaries and have equal decision-making power. Our board is composed of twelve women, eight African American, one Asian, and three white, with the staff ratio 50/50. Out of sixteen women on the board and staff, five are lesbians, four are over 50, half are rural, and most are working-class. Where we are weak is in our development of participation by youth and of women of color other than African American.

• **Changing the Agenda**. Increasing numbers of historically underrepresented groups gives an organization integration or diversity, but it does not necessarily bring about a shift in power. One of the ways we have tried to bring about this shift is to equalize access to decision-making. We believe that when there are predominantly women of color on the staff and board and everyone has equal say in the decision-making, then the agenda and how resources are used to support it will change.

Much responsibility is required: knowing about all aspects of the organization, attending weekly staff meetings and quarterly retreats, communicating well, and talking through issues until group agreement is reached. Each staff member is a lead organizer for a portion of the work. It is her job to oversee the vision and strategy, to recruit volunteers and other staff, to keep the rest of the staff abreast of what is happening, etc. However, each staff member does some work on each project, not just the one she is responsible for. In an annual board and staff retreat, we assess the year's work and lay out strategy for the next year. The staff meets quarterly to do the same, and then at the beginning of each month we provide each other with a work plan for what we hope to accomplish during the month. There are constant opportunities for analysis, criticism, disagreements, and revision. In addition to a strong framework of meetings and exchange, we have autonomy and independence; we are expected to dream big, to take on hard personal challenges, to think on our feet and be creative.

If we were a much larger organization, we would have to modify this structure, e.g., have people meet together in smaller work or issue groupings. The principle would be the same: all should take part in the decision-making that affects their work and lives at the organization.

Our ability to do good work and participate fully in decision-making is affected by the opportunities we have to gain new ideas both from the local community and nationally. We constantly work to try to equalize the privilege of access. For instance, I spend a lot of my time traveling, making speeches, attending conferences, and doing strategic work with groups. Each trip gives me great opportunities to learn new ideas, to make contacts with helpful people. If others on the staff do not have similar opportunities, then the way we work and interact together is affected. We look for opportunities for everyone to travel, to represent the organization in meetings and conferences, to be spokesperson with the press. All honoraria go to the Women's Project. Our policy is to provide financial support for each staff member to attend one conference a year just for her own education, not as a representative of the Project.

• **Relationships**. All of what we do is built on a foundation of developing and maintaining strong relationships with one another. We not only work with each other, we know and care about each other's lives. In a world of entrenched racism, strong relationships between women of color and white women are not built overnight. There are many stops and starts and uneven, rough terrain to cross.

One very difficult issue in the work to create equality is that of white privilege. What is one to do with the privilege that society gives a person simply because of the color of one's skin—so that when a white woman and an African American woman are together in public they are always treated differently? One cannot change the color of one's skin or society's response, but one can change how that privilege is used. It can be used—or spent—for oneself or on behalf of those who do not receive it.

"Spending privilege" is not just a matter of becoming an advocate and a friend, though those are important roles. It also means using privilege to make gains for others rather than for oneself, using it to open doors to helpful people, to sources of money, to information, etc. It means moving out of the way for someone else to be in leadership, be the face of the organization, be the major contact. It does not mean paternalism or off-and-on involvement in issues that are more crucial to the lives of others than one's own.

For trust to be built, those with privilege have to take great risks, putting the loss of that privilege at risk on behalf of the liberation of others. Why, for example should a black woman ever trust a white woman unless she sees that white woman is willing to take risks in the effort to bring about racial justice? A common slang expression is "you get my back for me," meaning I trust you to cover my vulnerable side that I cannot see or protect. That trust is not to be placed in someone who, when the bottom line is reached, is going to escape into her privilege to save her own skin. The rhetoric of race relations has to be moved into action. As white people we have to be traitors to the domination politics of our race. The same is true for all areas of domination. Heterosexuals, to earn trust, have to be willing to put their privilege at risk on behalf of lesbians and gay men, that is, by never hiding behind their heterosexuality and by being willing to let the public think that they are homosexual. Men, in fighting sexism, have to be willing to be seen as foes of male supremacy, as gender traitors, as not "real men," for that is how they will be attacked. People who believe in equality have to be willing to be identified with the oppressed and willing to give up their unearned privilege in the process. We have to be willing to go to the line for each other. Otherwise, we are dealing only with rhetoric and good intentions.

All of us constantly have to check the assumptions that come from our privilege. It is no easy task, but the reward of struggling for shared power and the elimination of privilege is the expansion of possibility for genuine friendship and the bond of common humanity. At the Women's Project, we seek friendships in our work. African American and white women, lesbians and heterosexuals socialize with each other outside the office. Much of our best thinking and work occurs in raucous, no-holds-barred conversations in the office hallway, around the copier, at the local blue plate diner. We joke, tease, disagree, fuss with each other, and talk, talk, talk. Our work is often enough to break our hearts, but we also believe wholeheartedly in fun, in the outrageous, in high waves of satirical response to the morning newspaper or the telephone call that pushed us over the line. Mostly, we believe that we have to bring our whole selves to these many hours we work together each day, that we have to be living the vision of the world we want to create.

• **Results**. Does it work? Not always. Sometimes we are overwhelmed by the murders of women we document, the entrenched poverty of so many of our constituency, the relentless racism, the reactionary legislature, the crack cocaine in our neighborhoods, the obscene greed of the billionaire Tysons and Waltons of our state. We do not always bring our best selves to the work. We have had our share of conflicts about race, class, and sexual identity. We have sometimes failed the community through lack of imagination or understanding of issues. We stumble. We sometimes move too fast without thinking through our strategy and possible outcomes.

Most of the time, however, it works. Our board meetings are day-long political conversations, with lots of food and laughter—we have to chase people out at the end. Even our most stressful days at the office are lightened by laughter and a sense of some accomplishment. Every staff member grows tremendously during her tenure with us and if she leaves, she goes as a strong social change worker.

But mostly we point to the work for our assessment. We think these policies account for our ability to get so much done with so few people and so little money. With our small budget and a current staff of four full-time and one part-time, we

• conduct an African American Women's Institute that works with women in local communities to develop leadership, to organize to solve community problems, to conduct political education;

• monitor racist, religious, sexist, anti-gay and lesbian violence, as well as the activities of the white supremacists and theocratic Right, document these activities and publish them in a yearly log, publish bi-monthly reports, work with community groups to do hate violence education and to organize against biased violence, work with allies to make public policy change, do political education about the economic and racist underpinnings of incarceration;

• produce written materials analyzing the Right, work with national groups to produce strategies to oppose them, provide political education nationally;

• provide incarcerated women with weekly sessions for battered women, work with United Methodist women to transport children to visit their mothers in prison, work with allies to change prison policies;

• publish an economic analysis of women's work and income in Arkansas; provide political education on economics; work with women in the Arkansas Delta on economic issues;

• provide HIV/AIDS education and training for women—especially lesbians, women of color, and incarcerated women;

• operate a lending library and a feminist bookstore;

• produce a bi-monthly newsletter of political analysis and opinion;

• operate a monthly women's coffeehouse, conduct a lesbian support group, produce women's concerts, organize statewide conferences and national strategy meetings.

The work is slow but it sustains us. It is hard but we draw inspiration from it. We recognize that every day we are struggling uphill against centuries of prejudice and injustice. We are all too aware that we do not have all the answers, but we are deeply convinced that we have a significant beginning. This is the only way we know how to advance a progressive agenda: to practice our politics as close to home as possible.

HOPE: CROSSING BORDERS, BUILDING BRIDGES

Sometimes the organization and expansion of the Right is almost overwhelming to me. It seems so all-encompassing that I waver momentarily in my faith that ordinary people with few resources can resist its destruction and build a just, liberating society. Then I recall those people who are pioneering new ways for people to work and live together. I am also sustained in my work by the examples of courageous people who are crossing borders into territory that traditionally has been inaccessible or forbidden, and of those people who are building bridges over divisions of fear, ignorance, and misunderstanding. They are pushing boundaries, seeking common ground, and opening new spaces for all of us to enjoy in our lives together. Their resistance to the limitations placed upon them and their willingness to enter uncharted territory often makes them endangered, but that resistance also offers us great hope for change.

Because the Right's strategy is to divide people and pit them against one another, we resist their organizing best by making real our vision of bringing people together to share common ground that is liberating for all of us. There are many examples of people traversing difficult territory to open a place for all of us to thrive. One of my favorites is Billings, Montana in 1993, when the community organized together to create safety for its Jewish, African American and Native American members. For some time there had been an increase in Klan activity in the area. During a Martin Luther King birthday rally, people found anti-King leaflets on their cars, and hateful flyers about lesbians and gay men had been posted around town. Though there were no direct linkages to the Klan, it was in this charged atmosphere that rocks were thrown through windows displaying Hanukkah decorations. A community coalition, made up of many different groups, individuals, and a large number of Christian churches, was created to respond. They persuaded the Billings *Gazette* to print a full-page picture of a menorah and encouraged people to put it in their windows. More rocks were thrown through windows that posted the picture, including one into the window of the Methodist church. In response, even more people put menorahs in their windows—an estimated 10,000. The vandalism stopped.

In another instance, when swastikas and the words "Die Indian" were spray-painted on a Native American woman's house, 30 members of the local Painters' Union and other volunteers painted her house. When skinheads began attending the African American Episcopal church, people of different races and religious backgrounds began attending services to block the skinheads' effort to intimidate. Working together in coalition, people sent the message that Billings was a town of open borders, a place of acceptance and inclusion.

Common ground and strong working relationships can develop when people who are very different from one another have time to explore both their differences and their commonalities in a setting that supports equality. In 1991, I was privileged to be an organizer of a dialogue on violence against women at the Blue Mountain Center in upstate New York. We focused on creating an analysis of violence which integrated race, class, gender, and sexuality. Of the 30 participants, 6 were African American, 6 Latina, 6 Native American, 6 Asian, and 6 white. For some of us white women, it was the first time we had been treated as part of a race numerically equal to other races and given no more than our proportionate time and space. The experience was profoundly moving. What was most exciting were the changes in the content of the discussion as everyone had an opportunity to speak the truth of her experience. Many of us had entered the conversation thinking we had a strong integrated analysis, but as we spoke of our commonalties and especially our differences a far broader and deeper analysis emerged. Of equal importance, however, were the relationships the thirty participants forged. I have fond memories of watching the Latina participants leading women in new dances late into the night, but my favorite memory of all is of twenty or so women sitting around the long dining table roaring with laughter as both heterosexuals and lesbians ranked themselves on the infamous "butch/femme" scale and gave hilarious reasons for their ranking. Bridges were built.

Some of the most important bridges are being constructed by people who possess more than one identity and lay claim to more than one world: multi-racial youth who refuse to be categorized into only one racial identity; transsexual, transgender and bi-sexual individuals who struggle with both heterosexuals and lesbians and gay men for recognition of their identities; lesbians and gay men of color who confront racism among white lesbians and gay men and homophobia among people of color. These people draw us into broader understanding of the complexity of who each individual is and the fact that identity cannot be harnessed, regulated, or coerced into restrictive little packages. Many times they are pivotal in our resistance to the Right's organizing.

With admiration I have watched Mandy Carter lead the National Call to Resist, an effort to counter the Right's organizing within African American communities. Mandy works with other African American lesbians and gay men to create bridges of dialogue and understanding, especially within African American churches that have been a primary target of the Right. As the Right tries to stir up homophobia and division within these churches, African American lesbians and gay men speak from the congregation and the pulpit to expose the strategies of scapegoating and division.

One of the most successful and loathsome strategies of the Right is the exploitation of people's concern for children and the family. Yet it is in this realm that I feel some of my greatest hope. No matter how hard the Right works to return us to a nostalgic notion of families, there is an unorganized alternative movement that continues to redefine and broaden the idea of what a family is and how it functions. There is no longer a tight border around families. There are blended families in which couples bring together children and relatives from previous marriages, families with single parents or two parents that are not married, families of gay men or lesbians and their children from prior or present relationships, adult children caring for their parents, single or married parents with adopted children, families of grandmothers caring for their grandchildren, chosen families such as circles of beloved friends or of those who provide support for the ill or dying. These families are not defined by a formula that requires a married man and woman plus children, but instead by relationships that are marked by mutual responsibility, common concern, shared interests, and commitment to one another.

Some of my strongest hope comes from two experiences of family in my own life where demands for change have been made and borders have been crossed, opening up ways to live more fully as whole people. My relationship with my uncle and aunt, George and Mary Pharr, now 87 and 80 respectively, has been a beacon of hope for social change. During the several decades since I first told them I was a lesbian, their willingness to address homophobia has enabled me to draw them fully into my life, and this has brought significant gains for all of us. Because of this openness, they share a wide community of my friends and their experiences, and I have beloved family involved in every aspect of my life. We visit each other, travel together, share books and recipes—their family and mine. We talk philosophy and sex, tell stories and jokes. Rather than the narrow lives of secrets and the unspoken, we have rich fullness of experience with each other. It is family built upon authenticity.

That truthful, open relationship has prevented these two rural, working-class people from becoming susceptible to the Right's organizing in their community. When people in their small United Methodist church began repeating the divisive messages of the Right, my aunt stood up and confronted them from the pew. She told them in no uncertain terms that she knew many lesbians and gay men, her niece among them, and that she admired them and the lives they lived. At other times she has taken church members aside to talk with them about their comments and her own positive, direct experience with lesbians and gay men. The bridges we build one by one between individuals are the strongest, as we can see from the polls indicating that the people less likely to condemn homosexuals are those who know a lesbian or gay man.

The idea of family expanded greatly for me when my former lover, Ann Gallmeyer, diagnosed with an inherited terminal disease, came to live her final years with me. Lovers for almost a decade and good friends for over two more, we had a lifelong commitment to each other. The demands of Ann's illness led us to remember our experiences with the women's health movement in the 1970s when we created care circles to surround those who were dying. We combined these memories with new information gained from gay men who cared for those living and dying with AIDS, and we created a care team for Ann. Though some came to the team because they knew one of us, all joined because they shared a common commitment to lesbians and an understanding of how difficult health care is for a lesbian dying in a homophobic world. Over several years, this team of 10 women became extended family to Ann.

We benefited greatly from our work with each other, but so did health care providers as we presented ourselves as open lesbians who made a family of support. When the time came for Ann to enter a nursing home in Portland, Oregon, we interviewed staff at almost a dozen homes, asking each about their social policies concerning lesbians. In almost every instance, there was a shocked response, with a quick answer that they had no problems with lesbians and that they had never had one in their facility—or that "what people do privately is their business." This provided us an opportunity for conversation about lesbian lives. At the home Ann chose, we led many of the staff away from the irrational fear that they would contract AIDS from touching Ann to an appreciation of the large gay freedom flag flying proudly on her door and of us as family that came visiting every day.

When Ann entered hospice care, one of our most emotional moments was when we realized we were honored as a legitimate family for Ann and that our relationship was respected for the depth of love and commitment that we brought to our care for her and each other. We took a moment to acknowledge that those bridges had been built by gay men and their lovers and friends who had gone before us in this beautiful place of comfort for the dying and their families.

Mrs. Daisy Bates, mentioned earlier in this book, has long been a source of hope for me. I lived for ten years in a house across the street from Central High School in Little Rock, Arkansas, where Mrs. Bates led the drive for integration in 1957. Every day I could sit on my screened porch and look across the garden at a rainbow of kids entering a fully integrated high school that is one of the best in the U.S. Looking at that school made me think about how for 15 years my life has been privileged by Mrs. Daisy Bates, a friend, a mentor, and a member of the Women's Project.

Then, in 1992, while I was away working against the theocratic Right in Oregon, I called my office one day and heard this story of hope and vision: There had been a small gathering of friends at my house overlooking Central High School where three of us then lived, white and middle-aged, African American and young, white and living in a wheelchair. At this dinner of friends, there were five lesbians, three white and two African American, and Mrs. Daisy Bates in her wheelchair, all eating Chinese food together and watching a slide show about Mrs. Bates' life. Of these lesbians, one created the Women's Project's lending library of women's and African American literature, another was an activist for disability rights, one was writing a book about Mrs. Bates' life, another wrote poetry and incisive political articles about lesbian battering, and one spent her days working to end biased violence against people of color, women, Jews and Catholics, lesbians and gay men. All sat there together, eating and laughing and talking, sharing friendship and politics and common cause. Hearing about it I thought, this is a glimpse of what the world can and should be.

I also thought, this is a truly moral vision. The theocratic Right frames our political efforts in terms of immorality and offers in the place of politics a narrow moral prescription. Yielding this terrain to the Right, progressive people do not talk often enough about the morality of our own vision. Could there be anything more moral than the idea that all people are of equal worth and deserve justice and full participation in their society? Is there anything more moral than the idea that people are connected to and responsible for one another? I don't think so.

My life is sustained by visions of the inclusive, liberating actions I see around me: people who with great courage and imagination cross borders and build bridges into new territory where generosity, tolerance, empathy and understanding reign.

PIECES OF A PROGRESSIVE AGENDA

What we have learned from the failures of our past and what the present anti-democratic organizing teaches us is that we cannot separate the work against exploitation and oppression. If we do, we fail. A united agenda that intertwines economic justice and human rights offers the best possibility of building a strong political base for creating change. It is what we are lacking now, and all of the media political ads and sound bites in the world will not take the place of a politically educated and motivated grassroots base committed to a pro-democracy agenda.

To do this work we have to create local organizations who work in combination with national resource centers and are committed to the cause of participatory democracy. We can forge a vision and strategy from our core beliefs to create a movement for economic justice and human rights. It is not coincidental that these two areas are the Right's weakest. As noted earlier, when we talk about the redistribution of wealth upward over the past two decades, we are accused by the Right of fostering class warfare—when, instead, the war against working people has been launched from the corporation board rooms for years. This response is a sure indication of the Right's Achilles' heel. There is no honest way to defend robbing working people for the benefit of the rich, for the destruction of human lives in the name of well-documented greed.

For change to come about, we must continue to point out contradictions, let conflicts arise, and then organize around them. There are enormous numbers of disaffected people who are hurt deeply by the economic practices of corporations and of the Right which serves them. Almost everyone knows that the social contract between employers and employees has broken down; that no matter how much one gives to the company in time, labor and loyalty, the company will not be loyal in return. Jobs will be eliminated, companies will move to cheaper labor markets, work will be doubled for less pay, workers will be made part-time. Everyone from the unemployed factory worker to the fast food minimum wage worker to the middle manager is feeling this crunch and beginning to understand it. We must speak to the sense of injury and injustice that workers experience, name the cause of their mistreatment, and present a strategy for change.

"Owner/manager/worker" class analysis does not fit easily; our organizing also must be around the broader issues of economic justice and economic democracy. Working people, the unemployed, and the poor are poised to enter a movement that fights for them. Unfortunately, at the moment, it is the Right that is most successfully organizing many of them using the issue of scapegoating and anti-government sentiment (the latter being another form of scapegoating since the government is negatively identified as promoting the rights of women, people of color, poor people and the environment over "true Americans").

We must give people a vision of hope and possibility, renewing their belief in participatory democracy as an alternative to the Right's agenda of exclusion. In our organizing for social change, we have to be intentional in our work to prevent the development of a new fascism.

Here are some strategies. End the social chaos in our communities which makes people willing to accept authoritarianism and the loss of their democratic rights as an answer to their desperate problems. Create a strong economy that offers secure, decent employment for all workers, with livable wages and full benefits. Intensify our efforts to defend and protect those who are the targets of scapegoating. Expose and oppose the leaders of the repressive movement and their policies.

These strategies can be incorporated into an overall agenda that works against fascism and promotes democracy:

• **Human Rights**. Place what is happening to people in this country in a human rights framework and link it to human rights struggles in other countries. Organize to hold the U.S. government accountable for its human rights abuses both in this country and internationally. Demand that it sign and comply with international human rights agreements and treaties. Expand our understanding of human rights to include food, clothing, shelter, livable income, education, and safety. Work for these by creating, for example, publicly funded child care, affordable housing, a guaranteed income. Direct public attention to the human rights abuses found in the U.S.—for example, in violence against women and in the U.S. system of incarceration. Work on the barriers and oppressions that prevent access to human rights.

• **Economic Democracy**. Organize to hold corporations and the government accountable for economic decisions that hurt the poor and help the rich. Demand that corporations put money back into salaries, production, development, and job creation. Point to the contradictions between salaries of CEO's, corporate profits, and salaries of workers. Push for equal distribution of wealth as opposed to the redistribution of the past twenty years that has sent wealth upward into the higher income brackets; support progressive taxation. Be prepared for red-baiting or accusations of fostering a class war when we talk about economic injustice; remember that the rich have declared war on the poor and we must call it what it is and defend ourselves. Accept no diversionary tactics, especially scapegoating, that keep us from looking at and changing the source of the problem. Broaden organized labor's constituency to include people in jobs and workplaces that do not lend themselves to traditional union organizing. Renew, overhaul, and rebuild the union movement, and work to change laws that restrict the rights of workers to organize.

• **Taxation for Human Needs**. Organize to demand a national budget based on fair, graduated taxation that will address human needs first. Through political education, help people understand that economics first represents a value system, and that the way a country (or person) spends its money is a reflection of its deepest values. Mount opposition to enormous expenditures on the military/industrial establishment and the use of the military as the primary job training program in the U.S. Insist upon a budget that reflects a desire to provide people decent jobs, benefits, and working conditions; healthy food and adequate shelter; publicly funded child care, universal health care, and education; and a safe environment. Demand, for example, a budget that spends more on education than on prisons. On the individual level, make equally difficult changes: end consumerism by practicing thrift and buying only what we need. Share our commitment to others by tithing a portion of our income to social change organizations to help solve the problems and meet the human needs of our communities.

• **Campaign Reform**. Work for elimination of the current form of "bought and sold" campaign financing, which depends on the contributions of corporations and the rich. Work for publicly funded campaigns which provide each candidate with the same amount of money and resources. Until this change is made, all of the other changes in our governing process will mean little. Campaigns will continue to be high-priced media shows lacking substance. Those who govern will still dance to the tune of those who paid their way.

• **Racial Justice**. Organize across racial lines to change the racist policies and practices of institutions. Develop political education that keeps alive an understanding of racial discrimination and injustice. Help our constituencies recognize that people of color are the focal point in the Right's development of the scapegoating necessary for the groundwork of fascism. For instance, confront and expose coded language such as the use of the words "crime," "welfare," "affirmative action," "under-class," "immigrants," "inner city," "gangs," "drug dealers" to mean people of color. This current attack is the continuation of a very old war against people of color, and once again it carries the potential for mass genocide. Link issues of discrimination and injustice.

• **Community-building**. Organize efforts on the local level to build and strengthen communities, emphasizing responsibility both to the community and individuals' rights. Develop ways to place multiculturalism at the heart of community life as the centerpiece of democracy. Strengthen the capacity of community organizations by developing political integrity which draws people toward hope and a desire for action, and which begins to develop a moral framework for our lives. Strengthen the capacity of individuals within the community by providing support for wholeness, for fairness, for generosity, for responsibility for oneself and for others.

• **Political Education and Grassroots Organizing**. All politics are local—work on the local level to provide accurate, truthful information and skills to develop a political base for change. Examine issues and policies in light of their impact on historically marginalized groups: women, people of color, old people, children, people with disabilities, lesbians and gay men, religious minorities. Work for the inclusion and leadership of these people in every aspect of local organizing. Make national organizations accountable to local organizations and activists. Develop individuals and organizations that exhibit political and personal integrity and provide hope. Create access for new activists and support their leadership development. Include young people in all of the work.

• **Longevity**. Create a pace that can be maintained for the long haul. This is ongoing work, not a short campaign that can be won or lost in one encounter. Be thoughtful about organizational and individual health. Create principled internal politics and healthy standards for work and working conditions. Be respectful of everyone. Do not act martyred. Build relationships that include more than work: celebration, ritual, play. Use positive humor whenever possible and often. Get a life, have a life, live a life—as fully and as joyously as imaginable.

The strategies and tactics learned from decades of movement building for social change still serve us well: direct action, media messages, political education, progressive candidacies, electoral campaigns, civil disobedience, study circles, voter registration and education, linkages through cultural/political events, the arts and the Internet, creation of alternative institutions, advocacy, legal challenges, and creation of activities and events that invite people to bring their passion for justice and put it to use. Organizing, organizing, organizing. However, as we know, tactics are neutral and can be used equally well to repress rather liberate a society. The central issue is developing a pro-democratic consciousness in those who participate in these tactics and strategies. We now seek ways to bring them into a vision of solidarity in the creation of a multi-issue, multi-racial, multi-cultural progressive movement that creates a democracy that works for all of us.

AND FINALLY...

We are living in a time of social, cultural, economic and political conflict in which many values are shifting and being redefined. It is a time of upheaval, change and fear of loss. Much of the conflict centers around what we believe the U.S. should be—a pluralistic (many ethnicities, religions, cultures), democratic society that finds a place and resources for everyone—or what the Right envisions—a mono-cultural, authoritarian society that puts tight limits on people's participation. Should we have a society that uses its resources for the common good or a two-tiered society with increased economic stratification and poverty? It is a conflict between the politics of inclusion and sharing and the politics of exclusion and selfishness.

At stake is the historical dream of this country and the values we seek in the ongoing struggle to make that dream real: that this country is open, providing a place where people can come in search of freedom; where people can find a place to be who they are and to live peacefully; where people can be equal partners with each other in the creation of family, community and government; where people have hope and resources to meet their basic needs.

We are living in a time of danger. Because of decisions made by corporate leaders in response to increased global economic competition, our standard of living has been in decline for twenty years. Concerted corporate effort to escape rightful tax responsibility and structural changes in the economy, such as automation, "downsizing," and sending our plants and production overseas where "underdeveloped" countries provide cheap labor, have accelerated the economic crisis in the U.S. during the past decade. Economic and social problems, coupled with a sense that a flawed government is failing the average citizen, make people seek answers in easy but aggressive right-wing populist solutions. People's fears make them susceptible to right-wing propaganda that tells them there are not enough civil rights and resources to go around. It could become the majority "will of the people," unchecked by democratic processes, that literally kills minority voices and rights. Economic hard times make people particularly susceptible to authoritarian leadership that scapegoats "minority groups" as the cause of social and economic problems. Worldwide, due to similar economic stresses bringing cultural disruption, there is a danger that regressive populism could slip into fascism.

It is a time when we must all be particularly vigilant that justice is even-handed, that all rights are equally protected, that there is equal access to educational and employment opportunity for everyone, and that we are careful to recognize and work on the complex causes of our social and economic unrest. Avoiding emotional, unexamined nationalism, we need to see ourselves as world citizens, and act as responsible stewards of the honored trust to develop and protect democracy and civil liberties. We must caretake and expand the moral ground of justice and equal participation in democracy.

As world citizens, we must find ways to end corporate imperialism and our government's support of human rights abuses when economic gain is at stake. We must hold our government accountable as a participant in the stewardship of the world's peoples, resources, and environment. A new definition of human rights (which goes beyond that of political torture or abuse to recognize food, shelter, employment, safety, education, health) must be held up as standard for people both of this country and of the world.

The work before us can be done one step at a time, beginning at the local community level and moving out to the international. Acknowledging the worth and dignity of every individual and developing an understanding of our vital connection to one another and to the natural world, we can create a society where children can be safe, healthy and educated; where people can have decent jobs that enable us to afford housing in clean, safe neighborhoods; where the rights and responsibilities of the individual and the community are balanced; where, worldwide, the health and well-being of people and the environment are considered the highest goals humans can pursue. Working together, crossing barriers and borders together, we will build a movement that makes real our dream of justice, equality, and freedom.

FUNDING FOR THIS BOOK

IN THE TIME OF THE RIGHT: Reflections on Liberation is a result of the Women's Project's commitment to providing political education to organizations and individuals to assist in their work against oppression and in the creation of a movement for social and economic justice. The work forms a circle that goes like this: We hold political conversations with activists and from these we develop our analysis, which we put into materials that can be used for political education; the money we receive from these materials, such as this book, we use to fund the work of the Women's Project—which in large part, consists of holding conversations and developing organizing strategies with political activists...

Therefore, this book serves as both an instrument for education and for fundraising.

Heartfelt appreciation goes to the following funders who saw the value of this work and provided the financial support for its initial printing and distribution:

ALBERT A. LIST FOUNDATION

FUND OF THE FOUR DIRECTIONS

PEQUOD FUND OF THE TIDES FOUNDATION

THE WOMEN'S PROJECT'S MISSION

All proceeds from this book go to the Women's Project to support its work to eliminate sexism and racism. Since 1981, That work has been guided by the following mission:

> Our goal is social change, or as the poet Adrienne Rich writes, "the transformation of the world."
>
> We take risks in our work; we take unpopular stands. We work for all women and against all forms of discrimination and oppression. We believe that we cannot work for all women and against sexism unless we also work against racism, classism, ageism, anti-Semitism, ableism, heterosexism, and homophobia. We see the connection among these oppressions as the context for violence against women in this society.
>
> We are concerned, in particular, about issues of importance to traditionally under-represented women: poor women, aged women, women of color, teenage mothers, lesbians, women with disabilities, women in prisons, etc. All are women who experience discrimination and violence in their lives.
>
> We are committed to working multi-culturally, multi-racially, and to making our work and cultural events accessible to low-income women. We believe that women will not know equality until they know economic justice.
>
> We believe that a few women working in coalition and consensus with other women can make a significant change in the quality of life for all women.

Also by Suzanne Pharr...

Homophobia:
A Weapon of Sexism

Homophobia: A Weapon of Sexism is perfectly timed to help us comprehend and combat the escalating homophobia and racist violence that is the bitter legacy of the Reagan Years. Her writing is what feminist 'theory' should be: passionate analysis based solidly in a commitment to act.
—Barbara Smith, editor of *Home Girls: A Black Feminist Anthology*

CONTENTS—

HOMOPHOBIA: A WEAPON OF SEXISM
An analysis of why homophobia exists and the way it works.

THE EFFECT OF HOMOPHOBIA ON WOMEN'S LIBERATION
How homophobia stops our work.

STRATEGIES FOR ELIMINATING HOMOPHOBIA
Ways to begin to eliminate homophobia in our personal lives and organizations.

THE COMMON ELEMENTS OF OPPRESSION
The methods used by sexism, racism, homophobia and heterosexism to keep people oppressed.

WOMEN IN EXILE: THE LESBIAN EXPERIENCE
Internalized homophobia and strategies for setting ourselves free.

All proceeds from the sale of *Homophobia: A Weapon of Sexism* support the work of the Women's Project.

Available from:
The Women's Project
2224 Main Street
Little Rock, AR 72206
voice 501-372-5113 / fax 501-372-0009
e-mail wproject@aol.com

$ 9.95

ABOUT CHARDON PRESS

Founded in 1988 by Kim Klein and Nancy Adess, Chardon Press publishes works relating to or funding the work of social justice and social change.

On Fundraising

Grassroots Fundraising Journal
(6 issues annually)
Grassroots Grants: An Activist's Guide to Proposal Writing
Andy Robinson (1996)
Fundraising for Social Change, Third Edition
Kim Klein (1995)

Of General Interest

Volver a Vivir/ Return to Life
PROJIMO/Suzanne Levine, ed. (1996)
The Family Guide to the Point Reyes Peninsula
Karen Gray (1996)
Naming Our Truth: Stories of Loretto Women
Ann Patrick Ware, ed. (1995)
Homophobia: A Weapon of Sexism
Suzanne Pharr (1988)
Home on the Range: Recipes from the Point Reyes Community
Foreward by Ed Brown (1988)

Chardon Press
P.O. Box 11607
Berkeley, CA 94712